Great
WATERWAYS
JOURNEYS

20 glorious routes circling
England, by canal and river

Coles Nautical
Bloomsbury Publishing Plc

re   1385 Broadway
            New York
            NY 10018
            USA

www.bloomsbury.com

ADLARD COLES, ADLARD COLES NAUTICAL
and the Buoy logo are trademarks of
Bloomsbury Publishing Plc

First published 2015

© Derek Pratt, 2015

Maps © John Plumer, 2015

Derek Pratt has asserted his right under the Copyright, Designs and Patents Act,
1988, to be identified as Author of this work.

British Library Cataloguing-in-Publication Data

A catalogue record for this book is available from the British Library.

Library of Congress Cataloguing-in-Publication data has been applied for.

ISBN: PB: 978-1-4729-0583-3
ePDF: 978-1-4729-0585-7
ePub: 978-1-4729-0584-0

2 4 6 8 10 9 7 5 3 1

Designed by Nicola Liddiard, Nimbus Design

Printed and bound in China by Toppan Leefung Printing

Bloomsbury Publishing Plc makes every effort to ensure that the papers used in the manufacture of
our books are natural, recyclable products made from wood grown in well-managed forests. Our
manufacturing processes conform to the environmental regulations of the country of origin.

To find out more about our authors and books visit www.bloomsbury.com. Here you will find extracts,
author interviews, details of forthcoming events and the option to sign up for our newsletters.

Great
WATERWAYS
JOURNEYS

20 glorious routes circling
England, by canal and river

DEREK PRATT

ADLARD COLES NAUTICAL
BLOOMSBURY
LONDON · NEW DELHI · NEW YORK · SYDNEY

Contents

Introduction

'I never saw an ugly thing in my life: for let the form of an object be what it may – light, shade, and perspective will always make it beautiful.'

These were the words of the artist John Constable (1776–1837), whose landscape paintings often depicted scenes of the River Stour in his native county of Suffolk. Constable lived at a crucial time in England's history, when the building of canals was integral to the success of the Industrial Revolution. During this period, a network of more than 2,000 miles of canals and navigable rivers was constructed, allowing goods and raw materials to be transported between the centres of industry and the ports. When the railways took over that role the waterways went into a slow decline and, during the 20th century, increased road transport and the severe winter of 1962–1963 put the nails in the commercial-carrying coffin. Today, although the waterways carry very little commercial cargo, because of increased leisure activity there are more boats afloat than ever before.

This book describes a 780-mile-long journey along the waterways of England, beginning in leafy Surrey and ending at Bristol Docks via the hills of North Yorkshire. The industrial landscape of the West Midlands contrasts starkly with the moorland scenery on the Pennine Hills. The route takes in famous towns and cities such as Oxford, Bath and Guildford as well as passing through remote countryside in Wiltshire, Oxfordshire and Cheshire. Other places of interest are featured, including the Black Country Living Museum in Dudley and Cadbury World in Bournville, not to mention all the architectural wonders of the waterway scene from locks, aqueducts, tunnels and bridges to the unique Anderton Boat Lift in Cheshire. This journey also gives us an insight into the contrasting canal-building techniques of pioneering canal engineer James Brindley (with his meandering narrow canals) and Thomas Telford, who built wider and more direct navigations 50 years later.

The idea for this book came after looking at a large-format map of the inland waterways system and realising that most of England's canals and rivers are now connected, which means that it is possible to circumnavigate the country by waterway. Thanks to the recent restoration of the Rochdale Canal and the Huddersfield Narrow Canal, there are actually three ways of crossing the Pennine Hills between Lancashire and Yorkshire. For this book I decided to follow the Leeds & Liverpool Canal, which is the more northerly of the trio of Pennine waterways and the one that never closed. Each waterway on the route has its own distinctive character, so it made sense to divide the journey into 19 separate chapters, each reflecting the particular appeal of each part.

I have been involved with the waterways for over 50 years and took photographs for the very first cruising booklets produced by British Waterways in the early 1960s. This led to a lifelong love of and fascination with the waterways, as well as a collection of photographs that I present under the name Waterways Photo Library. The aim of this book is to spotlight the enormous diversity of scenery and topography of England's inland waterways and show how boaters, walkers and cyclists can use them for short enjoyable stretches … or go for the full circle!

LEGEND TO CHAPTER MAPS

═══════	canal route
───────	other canal
════×══	lock
══⊏16⊐══	lock flight with number
════≡══	aqueduct
★	place of interest
🍺	pub
·········•·········	rail line with station
═══19═══	motorway with junction
───────	A road
───────	B road
───────	minor road
▓▓▓▓▓▓	settlement
▒▒▒▒▒▒	woodland
───────	river

Coxes Mill

Chapter 1

RIVER WEY & GODALMING NAVIGATIONS

The Wey Navigation was built during a turbulent time in English history; King Charles II was in hiding and the country was ruled by Cromwell's Protectorate Parliament. The navigation was planned by local landowner Sir Richard III Weston, who died in 1652 before it was opened. The 15-mile waterway, which connects Guildford to the River Thames at Weybridge, has 12 locks and required about ten miles of artificial channel to be dug. A four-mile extension, called the Godalming Navigation, was added in 1764, and together the canals are known as the River Wey & Godalming Navigations. The Basingstoke Canal and the Wey & Arun Canal both have junctions with the Wey Navigation.

The waterway was prosperous for many years, carrying agricultural produce, flour, paper, timber and gunpowder on distinctive Wey barges. These were capable of carrying 80 tons and were built at Dapdune Wharf by William Stevens & Sons, who later owned the navigation. In the 1960s Harry Stevens, son of the original owner, passed on the ownership of the Wey Navigation and the Godalming Navigation to the National Trust. At the time, the last regular commercial traffic was still taking grain to Coxes Mill, but this ended in 1969 and today the river navigation is only used for pleasure boating. It is not dramatic in terms of structures or surroundings as there are no aqueducts, tunnels or long flights of locks. At Guildford the navigation passes through the centre of town, but otherwise it follows a peaceful rural course through the Surrey countryside.

The Godalming Navigation near Unstead Bridge in Shalford.

Godalming to Guildford

Our long journey begins at Godalming Wharf, which is the most southerly point on the linked waterway network. The town has been an important trading place since the Middle Ages, as it is approximately halfway between London and Portsmouth. The arrival of the navigation in 1764, with its water link to London, only added to the town's importance. Today, the only original surviving building at Godalming Wharf is a barn that was built in 1768. The wharf once had 10 acres of warehouses – a huge area that has now been considerably reduced by the presence of supermarkets and car parks. Commercial traffic ceased in 1925 and now both public trips and private charters on a horse-drawn narrowboat can be made from here in the summer months.

Catteshall Lock, situated about half a mile from the wharf, has the distinction of being the most southerly lock on the linked waterway system. It stands next to a boatyard where boats can be hired weekly or by the day. Between Godalming and Shalford there are two miles of gently winding navigation flanked by woodland and meadows, where the only interruption is Unstead Lock.

At Shalford you will see the entrance to the derelict Wey & Arun Canal. This area is known as Gun's Mouth Junction

ABOVE **Godalming Wharf. The boat in the foreground is available for horse-drawn passenger trips during the summer months.**

BELOW **'Buddy' the boat horse pulling the public trip boat *Iona* away from Godalming Wharf.**

because of the presence of the former gunpowder wharves on each side of this entrance. Until the mill's closure in 1920, cargoes of gunpowder were taken by barge from Chilworth Gunpowder Mills to Woolwich Arsenal and Purfleet. Often called 'London's lost route to the sea' as it comes out at Littlehampton, the Wey & Arun Navigation (built in 1816) has been derelict for many years but is slowly being restored.

Soon, the ruins of St Catherine's Chapel can be seen on top of a high wooded hill overlooking the navigation. The chapel was built in the 14th century and was the subject of a painting by JMW Turner in 1830. A footbridge marks the former crossing point of St Catherine's Ferry, which was part of the Pilgrim's Way. It is a steep climb to the top, but the superlative views across the countryside towards Guildford make it a worthwhile effort.

There is a lot to see in Guildford both by the waterside and in the town, which is best accessed from Millmead Lock or the Town Bridge. In his *Rural Rides* William Cobbett described Guildford as 'a most agreeable and happy looking

Peaceful mooring at Shalford Meadows. The entrance to the Wey & Arun Canal is nearby.

St Catherine's Chapel, overlooking
the Godalming Navigation and the
countryside around Guildford.

town'. That was in 1830, but most visitors today will probably agree with this statement. At Guildford Wharf an old treadwheel crane was last used for loading barges in 1908.

River cruises are available from Guildford Boathouse near Millmead Lock, which marks the boundary of the River Wey & Godalming Navigations. The Yvonne Arnaud Theatre and Debenham's store both have cafes overlooking the waterside, where you can sit and watch the boats pass by. At Dapdune Wharf the National Trust visitor centre has a series of exhibitions, models and displays about the River Wey & Godalming Navigations. These include *Reliance*, a restored Wey barge that was built at Dapdune Wharf in 1932 and worked between Guildford and the London Docks until 1968. Guildford Cathedral, set in 20 acres of parkland, can be seen on a hilltop close to Dapdune Wharf.

Back at the town centre you can visit Guildford Castle. The original castle was built in the 11th century and became the royal residence of Henry III until his death in 1272. It then went into decline and became a private residence. It was purchased by Guildford Council in 1885. Today it has a visitor centre, beautiful gardens and a memorial to Lewis Carroll. On the steep High Street, which drops down to the river, stands the Tudor Guildhall with its overhanging bracket clock made in 1685. Also on the High Street is the Guildford House Gallery which has many fine paintings.

Alice's Adventures in Wonderland

A tribute to author Lewis Carroll (who lived and died in Guildford) can be seen at Millmead. It is a bronze statue of Alice with her sister, depicting the opening scene of *Alice's Adventures in Wonderland*.

Picnicking with her sister, Alice sees the rabbit who is about to lead her to her adventures in Wonderland.

Guildford to Weybridge

Leaving Guildford, parks and light industry are gradually replaced by houses with gardens stretching down to the waterside. The navigation takes a sharp turn after Bower's Lock and another at Broad Oak Bridge. The land between the bends borders Sutton Place, a Tudor mansion built around 1525, and the home of American industrialist Paul Getty, who died here in 1976.

By Triggs Lock there is an attractive cottage surrounded by woodland and open fields. Until you look at a map it is difficult to believe that the towns of Woking and Guildford are so close by. The National Trust has their maintenance yard and workshops next to Worsfold Flood Gates at Cartbridge, where there is a pub and some industry. A beautiful two-mile section now follows where the navigation passes through open meadows with no road crossing until Newark Bridge.

The flint ruins of Newark Priory can be seen on the natural river opposite Newark Lock. The priory was founded in the 12th century by Augustinian monks, but the ruins stand on private property and are not open to the public.

Papercourt Lock with its stepped weir is probably the prettiest lock on the river.

Walsham Flood Gates stay open except in times of flood. A pleasant wooded section leads to Pyrford Lock and The Anchor, a popular waterside pub.

The Royal Horticultural Society's (RHS) Garden Wisley is a short walk from Pyrford Lock. The entrance to Pyrford Marina, which has most facilities for boaters, is just beyond the lock. Continuing northwards, the tranquillity of the navigation is soon shattered by the elevated M25 motorway, which runs parallel as far as the junction with the Basingstoke Canal. The Basingstoke Canal is 31 miles long and has 29 broad locks. It ends at Greywell Tunnel (currently un-navigable), and is derelict from there to Basingstoke.

After the junction the navigation parts company with the motorway and heads in a straight line to New Haw Lock, then on to Coxes Lock and Coxes Mill. The last of the navigation's commercial trade brought grain here until 1968. The mill has since been converted into apartments.

Leaving Coxes Lock, the Wey Navigation makes a sharp turn towards Weybridge Town Lock and enters the well-heeled town of Weybridge. Thames Lock, the final conventional lock on the waterway, is immediately followed by a stop lock that enables craft to pass through when the water level is low on the Thames. Walkers will have to leave the river at Thames Lock on the River Wey and follow signs through Weybridge to rejoin the river at the start of the Desborough Cut.

ABOVE **Newark Lock on a warm summer's afternoon.**

BELOW **Thames Lock entrance to River Wey Navigation.**

A Tudor pageant at Teddington Lock.

Chapter 2

RIVER THAMES
WEYBRIDGE TO BRENTFORD

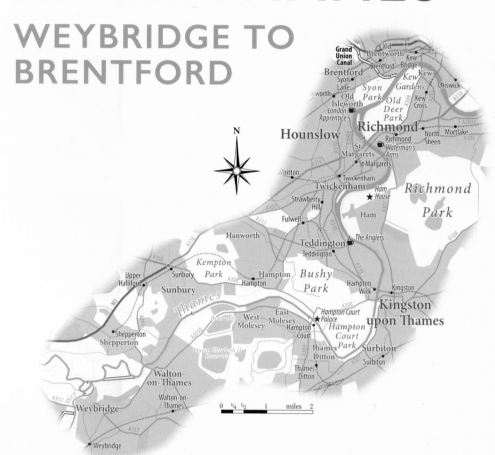

The Thames is England's greatest river. It is 215 miles long and is navigable for 190 miles. This section between Weybridge and Brentford is only 15 miles, but in that short stretch are some of the most famous locations to be found anywhere on the river; it could be described as an open-air museum of English history and culture. Great houses and palaces such as Hampton Court, Syon House and Ham House grace its banks, while towns such as Richmond upon Thames and Kingston upon Thames have become magnets for Londoners seeking a day out by the riverside. The river, once a busy commercial artery, is now a playground for boaters, rowers and anglers. At the weekend, the towpath throngs with walkers and joggers.

Weybridge to Kingston upon Thames

ABOVE **The new Walton Bridge.**

BELOW **Footpath between Walton Bridge and Sunbury Lock. Sir Arthur Sullivan of Gilbert & Sullivan fame lived near here at River House.**

Leave the Wey Navigation and enter the Thames through a series of backwaters near Shepperton Lock. Turning right there is a choice of routes to Walton Bridge: take the dead-straight Desborough Cut, or follow the shallow natural river with views of Shepperton. Walkers will have to leave the river at Thames Lock on the River Wey and follow signs through Weybridge to rejoin the river at the start of the Desborough Cut. Just before the start of the Desborough Cut is D'Oyly Carte Island, former home of Richard D'Oyly Carte (1844–1901), the renowned impresario and founder of the Savoy Operas that hosted Gilbert & Sullivan operettas. Eyot House on the island is now a boatyard.

Over the years there have been six Walton Bridges, beginning in 1750 with a fine-looking wooden structure that didn't last long, but was the subject of a painting by

Canaletto. This was followed by another bridge in 1788, which inspired three paintings and some sketches by JMW Turner in 1805. After various incarnations (including one that was universally regarded as the ugliest bridge over the Thames) the latest bridge opened in July 2013.

A fine wooded section of river with a convenient pub leads to the pair of Sunbury Locks. The river scene opens out after the locks with wide reservoirs on one side and opulent dwellings with riverside gardens on the other. After Platt's Eyot, which also has a boatyard, comes Hampton with its fine church and Garrick's Temple dedicated to Shakespeare, a folly erected by the actor and local resident David Garrick in 1733.

Tagg's Island at Hampton was once owned by Fred Karno (1866–1941), the theatre impresario who discovered Charlie Chaplin. The hotel he built here in 1912 was demolished in 1971. The island now hosts a community of chalets and houseboats. After this comes Molesey Lock followed by Hampton Court Bridge.

Garrick's Temple and Hampton Church.

Hampton Court Palace

Hampton Court Palace is without doubt one of the finest Tudor buildings in Britain. It was built for Cardinal Wolsey in 1514 and appropriated by Henry VIII in 1529 after Wolsey fell out of favour with the monarch. Henry lived here for many years and it was the home of five of his six wives. In 1689, Sir Christopher Wren was commissioned to enlarge and improve the building but most of the original Tudor features remain. The palace was eventually opened to the public by Queen Victoria in 1838 and has become one of the country's principal tourist attractions, along with its huge park and beautiful gardens, which play host to an annual flower show. The Long Water made for King Charles II, which stretches towards the Thames, is reminiscent of the Grand Canal at Versailles. One of Hampton Court's most famous features is its maze, immortalised by Jerome K Jerome in his book *Three Men in a Boat*. Another more quirky feature is the Great Vine, planted in 1769 and now reputed to be the oldest and largest in Europe.

After Hampton Court Bridge, there is a sweeping two-mile bend to the south with the wide expanse of Hampton Court Park on one side and Thames Ditton on the other. The park ends near Kingston Bridge while Thames Ditton blends into the town of Kingston. Seven Anglo-Saxon kings were crowned at Kingston, which gives a clue to the derivation of the town's name, and the Coronation Stone can be seen outside the Guildhall in the centre of the town. Another site of interest is the 12th-century Clattern Bridge over the little Hogsmill River, which is situated close to the marketplace.

Kingston was probably the last place in England to employ the ducking stool, a contraption that was used for punishing women by strapping them down and lowering them three times into the river. The last recorded use of this device occurred here in 1745, when a local innkeeper's wife was ducked for scolding in front of 2,000 witnesses. Kingston town centre, with its shops, banks and train station, is very close to the river and indeed the large John Lewis store is actually next to Kingston Bridge. Boat trips to Hampton Court and Richmond can be taken from Town End Pier.

The great gatehouse entrance to Hampton Court Palace.

LEFT View of Hampton Court Palace from the riverside gardens. This facade was built by Sir Christopher Wren for King William and Queen Mary.

CENTRE LEFT Inside the main marquee at the RHS Hampton Court Palace Flower Show.

BELOW LEFT The *Yarmouth Belle* is a passenger boat based at Kingston. Originally it worked at Great Yarmouth as a paddle steamer but was converted to diesel in 1947. The paddle wheel and funnel are now purely decorative.

BELOW The Coronation Stone outside the Guildhall at Kingston upon Thames.

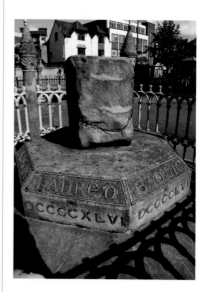

Kingston upon Thames to Richmond upon Thames

ABOVE **The Monty Python plaque at Teddington Lock.**

BELOW **A passenger boat leaves Teddington Lock. All three lock chambers can be seen in the background.**

Between Kingston and Teddington the riverbank is lined with sailing and rowing clubs. Teddington Lock marks the boundary where the river becomes tidal and the administration changes from the Environment Agency to the Port of London Authority.

There are three chambers at the lock. The barge lock is 650 feet long, the launch lock is 177 feet long and the skiff lock is just 49 feet long. The lock is manned and there are traffic-light controls for boats. Boaters heading downstream towards Richmond must take advice from the lock-keeper at Teddington about tide times and make appropriate bookings. Look out for the blue plaque that commemorates the famous Monty Python sketch 'Fish-Slapping Dance'.

A pleasant green section of the river, dotted with more rowing clubs, leads to Eel Pie Island at Twickenham. In the 1960s the Eel Pie Island Hotel (now closed) achieved fame

and some notoriety as a venue for jazz and rock groups. York House Gardens (opposite Eel Pie Island on the Twickenham bank) displays a series of Italian sculptures of cavorting naked nymphs around a fountain.

A ferry service still operates between Marble Hill House on the north bank and Ham House on the south or Surrey bank. Marble Hill House is a Palladian villa set in 66 acres of parkland. It was built between 1724 and 1729 for Henrietta Howard, mistress of King George II, and it contains fine Georgian paintings and furniture and is open to the public.

Ham House was built in 1610 and is remarkable for its superb Jacobean interior furnishings, most of which remain intact to this day. The formal gardens include the oldest orangery in Britain and an ice house. Ham House and its gardens are now owned by the National Trust.

One of the sculptures in the fountain at York House Gardens.

Richmond upon Thames to Brentford

Sir David Attenborough, the famous broadcaster and naturalist who has travelled to every far corner of the world, describes Richmond as his favourite place. The town retains the atmosphere of an 18th-century resort and its easy rail links to central London have made it a popular place for both Londoners and visitors from abroad. There are plenty of cafes, restaurants and pubs, especially in the vicinity of the elegant bridge. There is even a floating restaurant. The beautiful Terrace Gardens rise up from the river to Richmond Hill, where there is a famous view captured by many artists over the centuries. Carry on walking upwards along Richmond Hill and you will reach Richmond Park, which is the largest enclosed park in the Greater London area. Originally created as a hunting ground for Charles I, it still has a large collection of fallow and red deer.

Richmond Palace was first built for Henry I in 1125 (when it was known as the Manor of Sceanes (Shene)) and later rebuilt for Henry VII, who died there in 1509. Queen Elizabeth I also died there in 1603. All that is left of the palace today is its Gatehouse. This can be seen near

ABOVE **Watchful stag in Richmond Park.**

RIGHT **Terrace Gardens at Richmond.**

ABOVE **Richmond Bridge, built in 1777.**

LEFT **Walkers on the towpath near the Royal Botanic Gardens, Kew.**

Richmond Railway Bridge. Richmond Lock (a half-tide lock) and sluices are a little further along, beyond Twickenham Road Bridge. The lock and sluices control water levels upstream as far as Teddington. This barrier and its attractive footbridge were completed in 1894.

Now we are on the tidal river, passing Old Deer Park and Isleworth Ait on our journey to Syon Park. There is no direct access to Syon House and Park from the river, so boaters must reach it from Brentford High Street via the Grand Union Canal. Walkers must continue past the Royal Botanic Gardens, Kew and cross the river at Kew Bridge, then turn left towards Brentford and the canal.

Syon House was designed by Robert Adam in the 1760s, and is the London home of the Duke of Northumberland. It has a 200-acre park that includes a beautiful conservatory and a popular garden centre. There is a rather gruesome story that Henry VIII's coffin stopped here on its way to burial at Windsor, during which time it mysteriously burst open and his body was partially eaten by hungry dogs.

practical information

Distance: Weybridge to Brentford is 15 miles.

Boaters: Traffic lights operate at Teddington Lock. Leave Teddington for Brentford 20 minutes before high water. Arrival time at the lock must be within normal working hours.

Walkers: Good towpath with stations at Hampton Court, Kingston and Richmond.

Places of interest: Hampton Court Palace; Ham House; and Richmond.

Key pubs: The Anglers at Teddington Lock; Waterman's Arms at Richmond; and London Apprentice at Isleworth. Lots of other pubs en route.

Chapter 3

Two narrowboats sharing
a lock at Stoke Bruerne.

GRAND UNION CANAL

SOUTH SECTION

The Grand Union Canal (originally called the Grand Junction Canal) was built at the beginning of the 19th century as a shorter and more efficient route between the Midlands' waterways and London. Previously, all traffic coming from the Midlands had to use the winding Oxford Canal, transhipping their cargoes into barges at Oxford for a long, tedious journey along the River Thames to the capital. The Grand Junction Canal took a more direct route between Braunston and Brentford, cutting over 60 miles from the earlier Oxford Canal journey.

Map continues on page 36.

The new canal was built with locks 14 feet wide, which gave it a huge advantage over the Oxford Canal (whose locks were half the width at 7 feet) as it meant that two narrowboats could fit into a lock side by side. These wider locks could also accommodate barges, though with a limited range as the narrow-gauge system still persisted on the Midlands canal network. In 1929 the Grand Junction Canal was amalgamated with several neighbouring waterways to become the Grand Union Canal, and in the 1930s an attempt was made to increase the range for barge traffic by widening over 50 narrow locks between Braunston and Birmingham. Unfortunately, the scheme was never a success as the remaining Midlands canals were never in a strong enough financial position to be able to widen their locks. Although barge traffic was impossible beyond the Grand Union Canal's limit of navigation, the canal remained an important commercial carrying waterway right up to the 1960s. A British Waterways publication for 1957 states that a total of almost 1,000,000 tons of freight was carried on the Grand Union Canal in that year. Commodities included coal from the Midlands, as well as timber, grain, steel, cement and tar. Unfortunately, improved road communications and the severe winter of 1962–1963 – which saw the canal and its locks frozen, leaving boats immobile and crews helpless for several weeks – effectively ended commercial carrying on the southern Grand Union Canal. After that trade was very limited and the canal has now become a popular leisure waterway.

Milepost at Brentford. 'GJC Co' stands for 'Grand Junction Canal Company', which refers to the original name of the canal.

Brentford to Hanwell Locks

Brentford Depot was a hive of industry right up until the 1970s, although by then most of the waterborne trade originated from the Thames. The dock was surrounded by warehouses, most of which have since been replaced with modern apartments and a hotel. Syon Park, with 40 acres of beautiful gardens and a magnificent Robert Adam-designed house, is accessible from an entrance opposite the dock at the end of Brentford High Street.

Brentford is also where the main line of the Grand Union Canal begins. A tidal creek from the Thames leads to the Thames Locks, which are paired and controlled by a lock-keeper. Here you can obtain a licence to cruise the Grand Union Canal and all following Canal and River Trust (C&RT) navigations. Entry to Thames Lock is subject to the current state of the tide. All subsequent locks in the 93 miles to Braunston are self-operated.

Brentford Gauging Locks.

Leaving Brentford, the canal passes GlaxoSmithKline's huge glass office building and Boston Manor Park. Soon after this, the towpath changes sides at Gallows Bridge. This iron bridge was cast at Horseley Iron Works at Tipton in the West Midlands. The company was founded around the beginning of the 19th century and by Victorian times they were building fixed and moveable bridges all over Britain and abroad. Today, although structures of this type are very common in the Midlands, this is the only one on the southern waterways.

Six locks on the Hanwell Flight have woodland on one side and a long brick wall on the other, behind which are the grounds of Ealing Hospital. Halfway up the flight, by Asylum Lock, a bricked-up arch on the wall shows where there was once a short arm for boats to take coal and supplies into a mental hospital.

Beyond the top lock is Three Bridges, which is an unusual intersection of road, canal and railway.

Gallows Bridge at Osterley.

Bulls Bridge to Rickmansworth

At Bulls Bridge the Paddington Arm of the canal leaves the Grand Union Canal's main line under an elegant white painted bridge. The Paddington Arm is totally lock-free on its 13-mile journey through London's north-west suburbs to Little Venice at Paddington, where it joins the Regent's Canal. Bulls Bridge was once an important stopping place where working boat families could attend to necessary chores while awaiting orders. The canal company had a repair yard and offices there, which later became a maintenance yard for British Waterways. It is now a large 24-hour supermarket.

Leaving Bulls Bridge the canal passes through industrial Hayes and Stockley Park to Cowley Peachey, where there is a large marina. The Slough Arm of the canal leaves the main line at a junction near the marina on a five-mile journey that ends at a terminus basin near Slough town centre.

After Uxbridge the canal finally shakes off West London's suburbia and heads out into open countryside to Denham. Denham Country Park has some lovely woodland walks and, at Denham Deep Lock, Fran's Tea Garden serves excellent cakes. A series of lakes (old gravel pits, now flooded and used for numerous leisure purposes) accompany the canal for six miles between Denham and Rickmansworth. This is a beautiful section of canal and at times it is difficult to believe you are still only a few miles from London. On a hillside at Stockers Lock, Rickmansworth, where the television series The Adventures of Black Beauty was filmed, you can almost see the eponymous horse still galloping across the landscape!

Autumn cruising at Harefield.

Rickmansworth to Berkhamsted

At Batchworth Lock in Rickmansworth, there is a Canal Centre in a group of old buildings, and another lock leads from here to the River Chess. Continuing northwards on the Grand Union Canal, the waterway passes through Croxley Green and by the edge of Watford. Ironbridge Lock near Watford is beautifully situated between Cassiobury Park and Whippendell Wood. Now the canal passes through the former estate of the Earls of Clarendon, who allowed the canal to pass through their land providing that the canal company built a special bridge in keeping with its surroundings. The result was the splendid balustraded Grove Bridge.

A heavily locked section of canal goes through King's Langley, where the Ovaltine factory once kept its own fleet of boats to carry its produce to London on the canal. Further on at Hemel Hempstead, the Dickinson paper mills (known as Nash Mills) and the town of Apsley relied on canal boats bringing in coal from the Midlands. The mills at Apsley have been replaced by housing and there is a new marina with a startling modern steel footbridge over the canal. In 2013 Hemel Hempstead was voted 'Britain's ugliest town' in a national survey, and although this may well apply to its town centre with its maze of roads and roundabouts, the town shows its best face along the canal.

Berkhamsted has three canalside pubs and a pretty lock. Also by the canal is the railway station and, rather unexpectedly, a totem pole marking the site of a timber yard that imported wood from Canada. The ruins of Berkhamsted Castle are nearby, and the town is also the birthplace of author Graham Greene, who wrote *The Third Man* and *Brighton Rock*, among many other books.

Entering Cassio Bridge
Lock at Watford.

ABOVE LEFT **Unusual boat decoration. Instead of conventional flags this boat seen at a rally at Watford displayed a selection of brightly coloured underwear.**

LEFT **The Grove Bridge, near Watford.**

BELOW **Berkhamstead Lock.**

Map continues on page 40.

Cowroast Lock to Milton Keynes

The long climb of locks that began at Brentford eventually ends at Cowroast Lock, where there is a marina. The name Cowroast originates from 'cow rest', referring to the fact that in medieval times cattle being driven to London used to be able to rest and graze overnight at this spot. It is also an area rich in Roman remains, many of which were discovered when excavations for the marina were being made. The canal has now risen 395 feet from the level of the Thames, which makes it higher above this level than the dome of St Paul's Cathedral is above the ground. This is the Tring Summit, and it runs for two miles through a deep wooded cutting. The cutting ends at Bulbourne workshops, which used to build wooden lock gates. At Marsworth, there are seven locks that begin their descent alongside a series of reservoirs.

Marsworth Top Lock.

Workshops at Bulbourne.

The Globe Inn at Linslade.

Marsworth

Marsworth was an important stopping place for the working boatmen, who called it 'Maffers'. It is also the junction of the six-mile-long Aylesbury Arm where a flight of 16 narrow locks lead to Aylesbury Canal Basin. The Wendover Arm, which is at present is only partially navigable, no longer reaches Wendover. Its junction with the main line can be seen immediately above Marsworth Top Lock.

After Marsworth the canal heads out into open countryside, with views across distant hills topped by Ivinghoe Beacon. Bridge 118 above Slapton Lock is close to the location of the Great Train Robbery of August 1963. Civilisation returns at Leighton Buzzard with a waterside supermarket, followed by a picturesque canalside pub at Linslade. The canal begins to meander as it follows the River Ouzel valley until it reaches Soulbury, where it straightens out with three locks in quick succession, overlooked by another pub.

Milton Keynes was designated a new town in 1967, and grew into a city as its population expanded, incorporating existing villages and towns such as Wolverton and Bletchley. Many of these locations were already linked by the Grand Union Canal, which became a linear park within the new city. After the lock at Stoke Hammond the Grand Union Canal enters the city at Bletchley. There is a shallow lock at Fenny Stratford but after that the canal is level along its 12-mile journey through Milton Keynes. At first it follows the River Ouzel valley and then the River Great Ouse, which it

crosses on the Iron Trunk Aqueduct just north of Wolverton. Many of the former villages (such as Woughton-on-the-Green) have retained much of their original character despite being very close to Milton Keynes' centre. The environs of the canal remain pleasantly green through most of the city, with waterside parks at Newlands and Great Linford. At New Bradwell the canal crosses a dual carriageway on an aqueduct built in 1991. It is overlooked by a splendid old windmill.

LEFT **Pennylands at Milton Keynes.**

ABOVE **Heron on the canal at Milton Keynes.**

Cosgrove Locks to Blisworth

The level pound through Milton Keynes ends at Cosgrove Lock. Cosgrove is a lovely village a mile north of Wolverton, and features an unusual horse tunnel beneath the canal, as well as the ornamental Solomon's Bridge. It is also the junction of the former Old Stratford Arm and Buckingham Arm, whose entrances can be seen by the lock. The first section of the canal is still in water and is used for moorings.

After Cosgrove there are five miles of lock-free canal passing through pleasant open countryside with only one road crossing. There is a number of attractive brick bridges (known as 'accommodation bridges') which are used by farmers to connect their fields. These are mainly pedestrian and not intended for motor transport.

At the end of the five-mile pound, seven locks lift the canal to Stoke Bruerne. This is the epitome of a canal village, with two waterside pubs, a double-arched bridge, a row of old terraced cottages and the Stoke Bruerne Canal Museum located in a restored corn mill, all overlooking the top lock. The museum has an excellent collection of canal relics as well as a shop and a cafe.

Solomon's Bridge at Cosgrove.

Jack James

The Stoke Bruerne Canal Museum opened in 1963 in a converted corn mill. Many of the original exhibits came from the personal collection of former working boatman Jack James. At that time Mr James was lock-keeper at Stoke Bruerne and the mill, which had closed, was an ideal location for Britain's first waterways museum. Charles Hadlow, a former Grand Union Canal engineer who also had a fine collection of canal memorabilia became the first curator, with Jack James as caretaker. Today's museum attracts thousands of visitors to see working models, videos and above all the story of the inland waterways and the people who worked on them.

Outside the museum, a passenger trip boat takes visitors to Blisworth Tunnel, which at 3,057 yards is the third-longest navigable canal tunnel in Britain, with its southern portal about half a mile from the village. On a holiday weekend the towpath between the museum and the tunnel is often lined with boats selling specialist products such as cheese, books, rugs, woodcarving and sweets.

Before the advent of steam tugs, working boats were 'legged' through Blisworth Tunnel by the boat people. This involved lying on projecting boards at the front of the boat and pushing the boat by 'walking' along the tunnel wall. In the 19th century the tunnel had freelance professional 'leggers'. One legendary figure known as 'Ben the Legger' was reputed to have spent over 40 years lying on his back in the dark pushing boats for a small fee.

The tunnel has no towpath so walkers must follow a path over the top. The tunnel is broad enough for two 7-feet-wide narrowboats to pass inside. Boats wider than 7 feet should notify the authorities in advance so that other craft can be stopped from entering at the opposite end of the tunnel.

At the northern end of the tunnel the canal emerges into a wooded cutting then enters Blisworth village. Evidence of the village's industrial past can be seen in the form of surviving mill buildings and a wharf, which is now a boatyard.

Jack James outside his cottage in Stoke Bruerne in June 1973.

The Canal Museum at Stoke Bruerne.

Gayton Junction to Braunston

Gayton Junction provides the solitary link between England's canal system and the extensive Fenland Navigations. A long flight of locks carries the canal's Northampton Arm to the River Nene at Northampton. After that there are 60 miles of river navigation to Peterborough, which connects to the Middle Level Navigations and then to the River Great Ouse, which passes through Ely and Bedford.

Beyond Gayton, the canal follows a winding level course for seven miles to Weedon, where in 1803 a barracks and military dock with its own short canal arm were built. There was also once a Royal Pavilion for King George III, built for his use in the event of an invasion by Napoleon. Some of the buildings still exist, although the area is not open to the public.

The long lock-free section that extends from Stoke Bruerne ends at Whilton Locks where there is a large marina. It is not the most peaceful place on the Grand Union Canal as it is squeezed between the M1 motorway and the mainline railway. Seven locks take the canal up to Norton Junction where the Leicester Arm of the Grand Union Canal heads northwards to Foxton Locks and beyond to the River Soar Navigation at Leicester. Whilton Locks, which are also known as Buckby Locks, once had a boatman's shop at the top lock where the decorated Buckby cans were sold. These water cans were very popular with the working boat people.

Two pleasant, peaceful miles follow before you encounter another long tunnel at Braunston. This one is 2,042 yards long and the navigation restrictions are exactly the same as those at Blisworth. Again, walkers must go over the top and wide boats must obtain permission to continue in advance.

Near Gayton Junction.

practical information

Distance: Brentford to Braunston is 93 miles with 101 locks.

Boaters: All locks are broad gauge and can be shared by two narrowboats. Thames Lock at Brentford is tidal and controlled by a lock keeper who can issue CRT cruising licences.

Walkers: The Grand Union Canal is a designated long-distance footpath.

Places of interest: Stoke Bruerne village with canal museum; and Berkhamsted Castle.

Key pubs: Far too many to list in detail but the Boat Inn at Stoke Bruerne and The Globe Inn at Linslade are outstanding canalside pubs.

Chapter 4

Looking down Hatton
Locks towards Warwick.

GRAND UNION
CANAL
NORTH SECTION

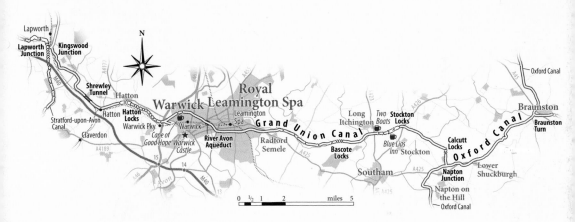

The northern section of the Grand Union Canal passes through pleasant
open countryside until it reaches Leamington Spa and Warwick. After
Warwick come 21 locks on the Hatton Flight and after these the canal
is lock-free until it reaches Knowle at the beginning of the Birmingham
suburbs. However, on this journey we leave the Grand Union Canal at
Kingswood Junction and approach Birmingham by another route.

Don't rush through Leamington Spa and Warwick as there is quite a
lot to see at both locations. A lengthy walk will be necessary as the canal
avoids the centre of each town, but places like Warwick Castle, along
with the Assembly Rooms and gardens at Leamington, make the stroll
worthwhile.

Arthur Bray

The Bray family carried coal between the Midlands and London, and a plaque dedicated to them can now be seen at Braunston Marina. The plaque refers to the 'Jam 'Ole Run', which was the boatmen's term for carrying coal from Atherstone on the Coventry Canal to the Kearley & Tonges jam factory near Bulls Bridge, Southall, in West London. The trade ended in 1970, but the journey is periodically re-enacted by a number of the original working boats.

Arthur Bray was born in the 9 x 7 feet cabin of his parents' narrowboat on the Grand Union Canal in 1905. He died in 1998, two days after his 93rd birthday having spent all his working life and retirement on a narrowboat.

Arthur Bray photographed on his boat *Raymond* at Braunston in August 1977.

Along the length of the Grand Union Canal there are mileposts that indicate the distance to Braunston. People who are unfamiliar with inland waterway locations often ask what or where Braunston is. Geographically, Braunston is a small village on a hillside near the town of Daventry in Northamptonshire. From an inland waterway perspective, it is the hub of the canal system south of Birmingham, where the Grand Union Canal and Oxford Canal meet. Leading canal-carrying companies such as Fellows, Morton & Clayton, Pickfords and Samuel Barlow (Tamworth) Ltd set up their boatyards and businesses here and so the village became a centre for the working boat people. After commercial trading ceased in the early 1960s, Braunston remained a boating centre for the leisure industry, with marinas and boat builders still in evidence.

The Grand Junction Canal became the Grand Union Canal following the amalgamation of several canals in 1929. These included the Warwick & Napton Canal and Birmingham & Warwick Junction Canal, both running northwards from Braunston. The two Warwick canals originally had narrow locks, which had to be rebuilt to broad-gauge standard after amalgamation. This involved making 52 new locks between Napton Junction and Birmingham, at huge expense to the canal company.

Braunston to Napton Junction

After leaving Braunston Tunnel, a wooded cutting leads to the first of six locks, which drop the canal down into Braunston. Although the old working boats have gone, Braunston still remains a busy canal centre with a number of boatyards and a large marina with an elegant Horseley Ironworks towpath bridge spanning the entrance.

A former toll office next to the bridge now supplies information about the village and canal. Every year, in the last week of June, Braunston stages an historic narrowboat rally, which attracts a huge gathering of ex-working boats.

Up on the hill, the village's single street is lined with shops and houses. The lofty spire of All Saints Church overlooks a graveyard that became the final resting place for many of the working boat people. There are pubs in the village and two by the canal.

ABOVE **Footbridge carrying the towpath over the entrance to Braunston Marina.**

BELOW **Braunston's annual historic narrowboat rally.**

BELOW **The Admiral Nelson pub next to Lock 3 at Braunston.**

BOTTOM **Boating near Lower Shuckburgh on the shared section of canal between Braunston and Napton.**

One of the pubs by the main road is also close to the junction with the Oxford Canal, which comes in from the right (see page 198). The junction consists of two splendid Horseley Ironworks bridges linked by a small island.

The 5-mile section between Braunston and Napton Junction passes through remote countryside, with hills to the south. Historically this is an interesting stretch because when the Grand Union Canal was established in 1929 there was a gap between the former Grand Junction Canal at Braunston and the Warwick & Napton Canal. The two canals were connected by the Oxford Canal, which allowed the Grand Union Canal to share its waterway – at a price! The Oxford Canal Company continued to extract toll fees from the Grand Union Canal until nationalisation in 1948.

The Grand Union Canal and Oxford Canal part company at Napton Junction, a place known to the working boatmen as Wigram's Turn. A large marina opposite the junction has adopted the name and is called Wigram's Turn Marina.

Napton Junction to Warwick

Turn right on to the former Warwick & Napton Canal and soon after passing a large reservoir you reach Calcutt, where there are three locks, a boatyard with a hire fleet and a marina. Then comes a flight of eight locks, which leads to Stockton. Here the old narrow locks are used as overflow weirs alongside the present wide chambers. The Blue Lias Inn at the bottom of the locks takes its name from the blue lias limestone belt that is prevalent in this area. Fossils and remains of prehistoric animals are often found in blue lias deposits, which explains the dinosaur that adorns the pub sign.

Stockton Locks was the site of a large cement and lime works, now closed. The cement company had its own private loading wharf called Kaye's Arm, now used by a community of residential boats.

The next village is Long Itchington, which has a village

The Blue Lias Inn by the foot of Stockton Locks.

Boating at Bascote Locks. The old narrow locks (now used as overflow weirs) can be seen on the right of the picture.

green and two pubs facing each other across the canal by the road bridge. The four locks at Bascote are a little further on. The top two locks form a staircase pair where one lock immediately leads into its neighbour with no intervening pound.

The canal now travels through open countryside, with the occasional single lock. At Fosse Wharf it crosses the Fosse Way, a Roman road that once linked Lincoln to Devon. Soon afterwards the canal reaches the outskirts of Leamington Spa.

The canal passes through a once-intensely industrial area of Leamington, filled with foundries and a gas works that used the canal for transporting coal. Much of the industry has gone and been replaced with housing, but there is still no hint of the beautiful Regency Spa town just along the road from Bridge 40. Leave the canal, turn right at the bridge and it is only a short walk to Leamington's many attractions, including the Royal Pump Rooms with its art gallery and museum, which is set in beautiful gardens next to the River Leam. The river also passes through the lovely and extensive Jephson Gardens.

Leamington Spa and its neighbour Warwick are separated by the River Avon, which the canal crosses on a three-arched aqueduct before passing through the north side of central Warwick, mostly flanked by housing. Cape Locks are alongside a pub called The Cape of Good Hope and shortly afterwards the Warwick & Napton Canal ends at Budbrooke Junction. The Saltisford Arm here used to be the start of the former Birmingham & Warwick Junction Canal and had become derelict, but it has since been restored and is used for moorings. This is the best place to stop and walk into Warwick to visit the castle and all the other attractions of this ancient town.

Warwick Castle

Warwick Castle was built in the 14th century on the site of an earlier Norman castle. The state apartments house a fine collection of furnishings and paintings, including a Van Dyke portrait of Charles I. Its dungeon features a display of torture instruments and its armoury boasts a helmet that belonged to Oliver Cromwell. The gardens, landscaped by Capability Brown, cover 700 acres and are backed by the River Avon.

A huge fire in 1694 destroyed most of Warwick's medieval buildings in the town centre. Much of what remains was built after that date, including the superb Collegiate Church of St Mary's and the Market Hall Museum.

Warwick Castle next to the River Avon.

Picnic by the lake at Jephson Gardens, Leamington Spa.

Warwick to Kingswood Junction

Very soon after leaving Warwick, boaters are faced with the daunting sight of 21 locks on the Hatton Flight. The sensible thing to do is to wait for another boat travelling in the same direction and share the work. The locks stretch for almost two miles and have a combined rise of about 150 feet. Warwick Parkway railway station is close to the bottom lock and connects with Hatton station, close to the canal at Bridge

Two boats in Hatton Bottom Lock, sharing the task ahead.

56. Walkers could take a three-mile route from Hatton station back to Warwick down Hatton Locks.

The views are a consolation for boaters, especially looking back towards Warwick. Another is a waterside cafe by the top lock and the nearby pub. A fine group of buildings that was once a maintenance yard overlook a pond containing a steel sculpture of a dragonfly.

For boaters it will be a relief to learn that there are over five miles of cruising before the next lock, and a visit to Hatton Country World is an interesting diversion that features an adventure farm, craft village, shops and a pub. To find it you leave the canal at Bridge 55 and walk south for half a mile.

From Hatton the canal continues through beautiful wooded countryside to Shrewley. Here it goes through a short tunnel, with an adjacent pedestrian tunnel used by boat horses in the days before engine propulsion. After Shrewley the canal passes along a steep wooded cutting to Turner's Green, where there is a pub called Tom O' The Wood in memory of a windmill of the same name that used to stand nearby. Kingswood Junction is a mile further on and this is where we leave the Grand Union Canal.

practical information

Distance: Braunston to Kingswood Junction is 25 miles with 46 wide locks.

Boaters: Two long tunnels at Blisworth and Braunston are wide enough for 7-foot beam narrowboats to pass inside but wider boats must get permission from the Canal & River Trust to arrange passage.

Walkers: There is a continuous footpath for walkers. Warwick Parkway and Hatton railway stations are both close to the canal.

Places of interest: Braunston canal village; Warwick; and Leamington Spa.

Key pubs: Notable pubs en route include the Blue Lias Inn at Stockton; Two Boats at Long Itchington; and Cape of Good Hope at Warwick.

Crossing the Avon Aqueduct at Warwick.

A wooded section of
the Stratford-on-Avon
Canal near Earlswood

Chapter 5

STRATFORD-ON-AVON CANAL

AND WORCESTER & BIRMINGHAM CANAL

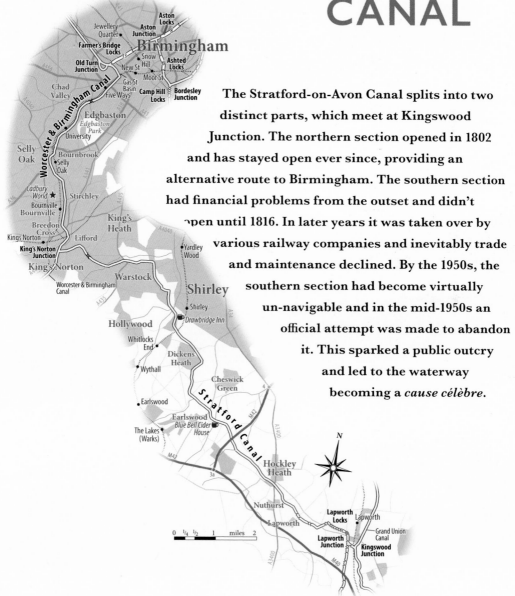

The Stratford-on-Avon Canal splits into two distinct parts, which meet at Kingswood Junction. The northern section opened in 1802 and has stayed open ever since, providing an alternative route to Birmingham. The southern section had financial problems from the outset and didn't open until 1816. In later years it was taken over by various railway companies and inevitably trade and maintenance declined. By the 1950s, the southern section had become virtually un-navigable and in the mid-1950s an official attempt was made to abandon it. This sparked a public outcry and led to the waterway becoming a *cause célèbre*.

In 1947, Tom Rolt announced that he intended to navigate along the North Stratford Canal. At one place near King's Norton he asserted his rights and the railway company had to jack up a fixed-swing bridge to allow his boat to pass by. This was widely reported in newspapers, gaining publicity for the newly formed Inland Waterways Association.

The National Trust acquired ownership and the canal's restoration began, with work mainly being completed by volunteers, army personnel and even prison labour. It was re-opened by Her Majesty Queen Elizabeth The Queen Mother in 1964 and the ownership passed to British Waterways (now the Canal & River Trust) in 1988.

This part of the journey follows the northern section between Kingswood Junction and Kings Norton Junction, where it meets the Worcester & Birmingham Canal.

The Worcester & Birmingham Canal is 30 miles long, has five tunnels, and is one of the most heavily locked waterways in the country. However, our five-and-a-half-mile section between Kings Norton Junction and Birmingham is lock free and there is just one short tunnel at Edgbaston to negotiate.

Boating on the Stratford-on-Avon Canal through Birmingham's leafy southern suburbs, less than five miles from the city centre.

Kingswood Junction to Kings Norton

In 1802 a short canal was built to connect the Birmingham & Warwick Junction Canal to the Stratford-on-Avon Canal, and this is where you leave the Grand Union Canal and continue the journey along the northern Stratford-on-Avon Canal. After a few yards there is a small junction where boaters should turn right into Lock 20 on the Lapworth Lock Flight. There is no problem for walkers, who just follow the towpath and cross the footbridge. Kingswood Junction is an attractive place bordered by woodland, with the Canal & River Trust offices and maintenance yard next to Lock 21.

Boaters are immediately faced with 18 locks on the Lapworth Lock Flight. All the locks are narrow gauged and easier to work than their broad counterparts on the Grand Union Canal. However, beyond Lapworth Top Lock there are no more locks, apart from one stop lock at Kings Norton, all the way to Birmingham. The 18 locks are crammed

Boats pass each other at Kingswood Junction. The boat on the right is entering Lock 21 (the start of the southern Stratford-on-Avon Canal) while the other boat has just left Lock 20 and is heading north.

BELOW **A split bridge at Lapworth Lock Flight.**

BOTTOM **Kings Norton Junction.**

together in the space of one mile, with a breathing space (including a canal shop and a pub) between Locks 14 and 15, and another between Lock 6 and the top. Lapworth Station, a short walk from Bridge 34, is on the same line as Hatton and Warwick Parkway.

The cast-iron split bridges here are typical of the Stratford-on-Avon Canal. The gap in the centre of the arch was to allow the towrope to pass through without unhitching the horse, when horsepower was the only propulsion for working boats.

After the top lock, the canal follows a north-westerly course to Hockley Heath where there are shops and a pub. Warings Green, two miles further on, has a renowned canal-side bakery and the Blue Bell Cider House pub. The canal then straightens out on a wooded cutting that leads to boat-club moorings at Earlswood. A series of reservoirs to the south attract birdwatchers and anglers and a partly navigable feeder brings water to the canal. Despite being so close to Birmingham's outer suburbs, this section of canal is wooded in places, and has a rural feel about it.

Boaters will require a windlass and a British Waterways (BW) key to operate the Shirley Drawbridge. You can enjoy a

drink at the adjoining pub while working out the instructions.

Although you are now in the residential outskirts of Birmingham, the canal continues its sylvan course oblivious to the commuter traffic that accompanies the waterway on nearby roads.

Brandwood Tunnel has the distinction of being the only tunnel on the entire canal between Kings Norton and Stratford-upon-Avon. It celebrates its rather tenuous Shakespearian connection with a bust of the immortal bard on its western portal.

King's Norton stop lock is unusual for its two wooden guillotine gates balanced by chains and counterweights. The machinery is no longer used and the lock remains permanently open.

The Stratford-on-Avon Canal ends at Kings Norton Junction where it joins the Worcester and Birmingham Canal, overlooked by a fine junction house with an interesting list of tolls dating from 1894.

Before leaving Kings Norton, consider a walk through the adjacent park to the church, with its imposing spire that is visible from the canal. The 15th-century Old Grammar School next to the church was the winner of the BBC's *Restoration* programme in 2004.

TOP **Passing beneath the Shirley Drawbridge.**

ABOVE **Family boating at Brandwood End in Birmingham's suburbia.**

Kings Norton to Birmingham

Cadbury World

Cadbury World opened in 1990 and tells the story of the Cadbury family opening their shop in Birmingham in 1824, before moving to their first factory in 1831. It also shows how chocolate is made and gives the visitor an opportunity to sample some of the products.

The Cadbury brothers moved their factory from Birmingham to Bournville in 1879 and began building a village for their workers in this rural environment, which was completely different from the inner-city slums most of them were living in at the time. They also provided leisure facilities, such as playing fields and playgrounds for the workers' children.

OPPOSITE **Wooded section between Selly Oak and Birmingham University.**

RIGHT **Cadbury World, with its children's playground and outdoor cafe in the foreground.**

Turn right at the junction and after a mile you'll reach Bournville station. There are visitor moorings here but no direct access to Cadbury World from the towpath. Visitors to Cadbury World need to cross the bridge over the canal and railway and follow directions to the entrance.

The position of the factory by the Worcester & Birmingham Canal was very important, and in the early days Cadbury relied on the canal for its supply of raw materials. For many years they had their own fleet of canal boats and were one of the first companies to introduce motors into their boats. They abandoned their fleet in 1929 but carried on using independent carrying companies for the transportation of chocolate crumb and other raw materials between their factories at Knighton Wharf on the Shropshire Union Canal, Bournville and Frampton-on-Severn. This service continued until 1961.

There are five miles of waterway between Bournville and the canals of central Birmingham. For most of its length the Worcester & Birmingham Canal provides a green passage through an intensely urban area, but first it passes through

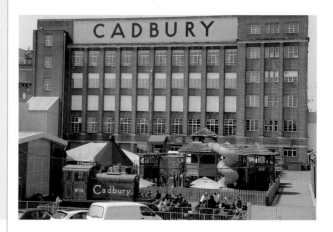

Selly Oak, with a busy road junction, large shopping complex and a railway station all close to the canal. Selly Oak was once the junction between the Worcester & Birmingham Canal and the Dudley No 2 Canal. This eastern end of the Dudley Canal has been closed for years following the collapse in 1917 of the very long and narrow Lapal Tunnel.

The canal then passes through a beautiful wooded section, flanked by the University of Birmingham, The Birmingham Botanical Gardens at Edgbaston and a large hospital. University Station is next to the canal. Edgbaston Tunnel is only 105 yards long and the towpath passes through it. Beyond the tunnel you will see the high buildings that announce the approach of central Birmingham.

At Holliday Wharf there is a very sharp bend to the left beneath a huge building called The Cube. This takes you to Worcester Bar and Gas Street Basin. Directly ahead is The Mailbox complex of bars, shops and restaurants built around the former Royal Mail sorting office.

practical information

Distance: Kingswood Junction to Birmingham is 18 miles with 18 narrow locks

Boaters: Boaters will need a Watermate key to operate Shirley Drawbridge.

Walkers: There is a continuous footpath for walkers. There are railway stations close to the canal at Lapworth, Bournville, University and Five Ways in Birmingham.

Places of interest: Bournville village and Cadbury World.

Key pubs: Drawbridge Inn at Shirley and Blue Bell Cider House at Warings Green.

Smethwick Pumping Station by
the New Main Line. The Old
Main Line is on a higher level
to the right of the picture.

Chapter 6

BIRMINGHAM CANAL

We begin at Gas Street Basin in central Birmingham
and follow the main line canal to Wolverhampton. The
route is mostly built up with occasional glimpses of greenery
among the relics of industry. Birmingham was established as a
manufacturing and industrial centre by the mid-1700s. Indeed,
Arthur Young, an eminent writer on economics at the time
described Birmingham as 'the first manufacturing town in the
world'. However, there was the problem of transportation: how to
bring in the raw materials and distribute the finished products?

Pudding Green Junction milepost.

Birmingham had no navigable rivers so the only method of transport in those days was the road network, which was primitive and often impassable during the winter months. This problem had been solved a little further north by Josiah Wedgwood, who had promoted pioneer canal engineer James Brindley's building of the Trent & Mersey Canal. Birmingham followed suit and its first Brindley-built canal opened in 1769, connecting the town with the coalmines around Wednesbury in what is now called the Black Country. Within a year the price of coal in Birmingham had halved.

Brindley pushed on and in 1772 Birmingham was connected to Wolverhampton Canal and the Staffordshire & Worcestershire Canal. This opened up routes to the Rivers Severn and Mersey and through them the ports of Bristol and Liverpool. A network of canals rapidly developed across the Black Country giving the region the title of 'The Workshop of the World'.

Brindley's technique was to follow the contours of the land, only building locks when unavoidable. Unfortunately, with the increase in business, boats on Brindley's winding waterways were taking too long. This prompted the arrival on the scene of Thomas Telford, who engineered the Birmingham New Main Line Canal, completed in 1838. Telford's canal was built in a straight line with embankments and deep cuttings, chopping seven miles off the previous length. Brindley's canal already served factories and foundries so it remained (to this day) as a series of loops from the main line. Both canals are known as the Birmingham Canal Navigations or BCN. They were hugely successful and even as late as 1888, despite railway competition, the BCN was carrying 8,000,000 tons of goods a year.

Our journey will follow Telford's main line to Wolverhampton, with a number of junctions along the way where some of the BCN's surviving canals connect to the main line. At times the canal passes through acres of decaying industry, where the bones of old factories and foundries conjure a melancholic atmosphere of the canal's working past. In other places nature has returned, carpeting the canal banks with a profusion of wild flowers.

Gas Street Basin to Smethwick

We begin our BCN journey at Worcester Bar, which is now a narrow strip of canal between the main basin and the canal beyond. Originally, Worcester Bar was built as a stone barrier between the Birmingham Canal in Gas Street Basin and the Worcester & Birmingham Canal because the two canal companies were in dispute about water supplies. This meant that cargoes had to be physically transhipped from one canal to the other until the companies came to an agreement and built a stop lock in 1815.

If you were not already by the canal you would never know Gas Street Basin existed, as the entrance is so hidden away it is invisible from the street. The basin was once surrounded by old warehouses overlooking the moored

BELOW **Worcester Bar today. A former toll house is now a canalside pub and cafe.**

Brindleyplace is a bustling centre with many shops, restaurants and bars.

residential narrowboats that gave the basin so much character. Most of the warehouses were controversially demolished in the 1970s and today the basin is overlooked by modern buildings, including the towering hotel Hyatt Regency Birmingham. At least the moored boats are still here, adding a splash of colour to the scene.

Moving on beneath Broad Street Bridge, we enter Brindleyplace with its restaurants, bars, shops, hotels and galleries. Pause awhile and reflect that before the 1990s this part of Birmingham's canal had degenerated to such an extent that it was no longer a safe place to linger, especially after dark. Many of the original buildings were in a state of collapse. Visit Brindleyplace after dark today and you will discover a lively scene bustling with people enjoying an evening out.

The International Convention Centre on the opposite side of the canal from Brindleyplace contains the Symphony Hall and hosted the G8 Summit conference in 1998. Move along the canal and stand facing Old Turn Junction where three canals meet and the National Indoor Arena is behind you. The National Sea Life Centre is on the right and the Malt House pub to the left. The pub achieved fame in 1998 when President Bill Clinton, having a break from the G8 Summit, stood on the pub balcony quaffing a pint of their best bitter. Old Turn Junction was an important turning place in the days of the working boatman, but he probably wouldn't recognise the scene today. All of these places are linked by several footbridges across the canal.

There is a signpost in the middle of the canal at Old Turn Junction and you follow the direction to Wolverhampton with the National Sea Life Centre on the left.

The entrance to the Oozells Street Loop can be seen shortly after the National Sea Life Centre. This is the first loop of Brindley's Birmingham Canal Old Main Line and is mostly used for private moorings. Very soon you pass the Icknield Port Loop on the left followed on the right by the

ABOVE **A waterbus passes the National Sea Life Centre.**

BELOW **Old Turn Junction with the Malt House pub on the left. The International Convention Centre and the Hyatt Regency Birmingham can be seen in the background.**

Birmingham's straight Main Line Canal at Winson Green. The entrance to the Soho Loop is on the left of the picture.

Soho Loop. If you follow the Soho Loop you will see Hockley Port Interchange Basin. This was a former canal-to-railway interchange and is now used for moorings. Also on the Soho Loop was Matthew Boulton's factory where Boulton and his partner James Watt developed the steam engine from being a primitive device used for pumping water to a source of power for industry. Soho House, a museum celebrating the life of this famous duo is now open to the public. The Soho Loop rejoins the main line at Winson Green.

When Brindley's canal reached Smethwick in 1779 it was necessary to build locks at each side of a hill. Locks use up a lot of water and there was no natural water supply so two pumping stations with steam engines were needed to pump water back to the short summit pound. These were built by Boulton & Watt at the Soho foundry.

The two canals split at Smethwick Junction where the Birmingham Canal Old Main Line climbs the three Smethwick Locks. These locks were actually built by John Smeaton in the 1780s, replacing six locks built by Brindley that ran at a higher level.

After Smethwick Junction, Telford's New Main Line goes into a deep cutting passing under the Engine Arm Aqueduct. This was built by Telford in 1825 to carry a branch canal from the Birmingham Canal Old Main Line that served as a water feeder from Rotton Park Reservoir. It also enabled boats to bring in coal to feed the Smethwick Engine that served the locks. The engine has long gone, replaced by the one in the pumping station at Brasshouse Lane; so too have most of the wharves and factories that once lined the canal basin.

In 1892 a new pumping station was built and still stands today between the two main line canals at Brasshouse Lane, Smethwick. The nearby Galton Valley Canal Heritage Centre explains all the history and problems involved in building the two main line canals.

ABOVE **A specially designed trip boat about to enter Dudley Tunnel.**

BELOW **The Engine Arm Aqueduct built by Telford crosses the New Main Line at Smethwick.**

Smethwick to Tipton Green

OPPOSITE **The canal forms an integral part of the Black Country Museum's village.**

BELOW **The Old Main Line crosses Telford's New Main Line at Stewart Aqueduct beneath the M5 motorway viaduct.**

In the summertime, the steep banks of the New Main Line cutting are ablaze with wild flowers, bringing a touch of the countryside to an intensely built-up area. At 151 feet, Telford's Galton Bridge was the longest single-span bridge in the world when it was constructed in 1829. Today, some of the visual impact of its span across the cutting has been lost by the building of nearby Galton Tunnel and a railway bridge. The New Main Line becomes really dramatic when the Old Main Line crosses it by the Stewart Aqueduct, which in turn is dwarfed by the towering M5 motorway viaduct. This meeting of transport routes past and present is completed by the railway that runs alongside the cutting. Bromford Junction lies just beyond the Stewart Aqueduct. This is where the three Spon Lane locks drop down from the Old Main Line. The New Main Line continues along its

The Black Country Living Museum is an open-air museum with a reconstructed Black Country village built around an existing canal arm. The exhibits range from the 1860s–1930s. The canal hosts a fine collection of ex-working boats including a steam narrowboat called *President*, which in the summer travels around the waterway system publicising the museum. Visitors can also take a boat trip into the adjacent Dudley Tunnel in a specially designed trip boat. The village's main street includes shops and a pub and is spanned by a bridge that was moved from Wolverhampton. The museum also has a colliery, workshops, a working replica of a Newcomen engine and a fairground.

Main street in the Black Country Living Museum village.

straight course, passing three more canal junctions. The first one is the gloriously named Pudding Green Junction, which leads to the Wednesbury Old Canal that was part of Brindley's original waterway to Birmingham.

The Wednesbury Old Canal now links to the Walsall Canal at Ryders Green Junction, providing an entrance to a network of canals in the Black Country. Albion Junction leads to the Gower Branch, which leads to another connection to the Old Main Line via three locks at Brades Hall Junction Bridge. This is closely followed by Dudley Port Junction, which leads to Netherton Tunnel and the Dudley Canals. Netherton is the third-longest navigable tunnel in Britain at 3,027 yards and has a double towpath running through it.

The New Main Line continues its straight course with bushes, trees and wild flowers softening the industrial background. It crosses a main road on the Ryland Aqueduct and then drops down the three Factory Locks to Tipton Green where it rejoins the Old Main Line that swings in from the south. Turn left on to the Old Main Line for a short while to visit the Black Country Living Museum.

Tipton Green to Aldersley Junction

Back at Tipton Green, the two canals have now merged into one and will stay that way for the rest of the journey to Wolverhampton. Once clear of industrial Tipton Green the canal passes along a pleasant green cutting to Coseley Tunnel. The tunnel opened in 1837 following construction difficulties caused by coal mining in the area, and has a double towpath.

After Coseley Tunnel comes the junction with the Wednesbury Oak Loop. This used to connect to the distant Walsall Canal but now ends after one-and-a-half miles at Bradley Workshops. The canal continues through a region where foundries and steelworks once lit up the night sky and assailed the ears of the working boat people with their deafening sounds. The journey is more peaceful today as the canal reaches Chillington Wharf, a well-preserved example of a canal-to-railway interchange depot. Next comes Horseley Fields Junction, which marks the start of the Wyrley & Essington Canal, which navigates around the northern fringe of the Black Country canals.

Lock 12 on the Wolverhampton Lock Flight.

Boating on Wolverhampton Lock Flight with Oxley Viaduct in the background.

You are now in Wolverhampton and boaters wishing to sample the many delights of the town centre should find a mooring by the landscaped area by Wolverhampton Top Lock. Here a warehouse once owned by the famous canal carriers Fellows, Morton & Clayton Ltd has been converted into a nightclub.

Boaters need to take a deep breath before tackling the 21 locks on the Wolverhampton Lock Flight. The working boatmen called them the 'Twenty One' and in those days young men and boys known as 'hobblers' would offer to help a single-handed boatman work the locks for a small fee. The first few locks on the flight pass through a very industrial area with a gasworks, a former brewery and a refuse incinerator.

After a section flanked with housing, the surroundings become increasingly open. The end of the flight by Wolverhampton's racecourse looks so rural it is hard to remember you are still only a couple of miles from the city centre.

Aldersley Junction comes soon after the bottom lock and here we leave the BCN and join the Staffordshire & Worcestershire Canal and then the Shropshire Union Canal.

practical information

Distance: Gas Street Basin to Wolverhampton is 24 miles with 24 locks, most of them at Wolverhampton. The New Main Line Canal is lock free from Old Turn Junction until the 3 Factory Locks at Tipton Green.

Boaters: Be aware of floating rubbish on this very built up section of canal.

Walkers: There is a continuous footpath for walkers. The railway from Wolverhampton follows the canal to railway stations at Coseley, Tipton, Dudley Port, Sandwell and Dudley and Smethwick Galton Bridge, all of which are close to the canal. These stations all connect to Birmingham New Street.

Places of interest: The main attraction is the Black Country Living Museum at Dudley.

Key pubs: There are lots of pubs near the canal in Birmingham and Wolverhampton.

High Bridge in Grub Street cutting.

· 39 ·

Chapter 7

SHROPSHIRE UNION CANAL

The Shropshire Union Canal
began life as the Birmingham
& Liverpool Junction Canal.
It connects the Staffordshire
& Worcestershire Canal at
Autherley Junction near
Wolverhampton to the much
older Chester Canal at Nantwich,
thereby opening a direct route from
the Mersey to Birmingham. Severe
construction difficulties delayed
the opening of the canal until 1835,
but after that it was commercially
successful for a while before being
affected by railway competition.

Previously known as 'The Shroppie',
the canal has become one of Britain's
most popular cruising waterways. It is a
canal where you can slow down and enjoy
the remote countryside. Just make sure you
have enough supplies in stock as retail
outlets can be few and far between.

Stretton Aqueduct, built by Thomas Telford in 1832, crossing the A5 trunk road.

The canal was engineered by Thomas Telford using a technique known as 'cut and fill', which maintains a straight waterway by building deep cuttings followed by high embankments. On our journey along Telford's Birmingham Canal Main Line we have already encountered this technique, but there the resemblance ends. Although the two canals are very close to each other, the difference between them is extraordinary. The Birmingham Canal Main Line passes through an intensely industrialised region whereas the Shropshire Union Canal follows a totally rural course through some outstandingly scenic countryside.

The journey from Autherley Junction to Barbridge Junction is 42 miles, followed by a further ten miles along the Middlewich Branch. For walkers there is a continuous footpath, mostly in good condition, although the towpath in some of the deep cuttings can be wet in winter so appropriate footwear and attire is a must.

Autherley Junction to Gnosall

Aldersley Junction is where the Birmingham Canal Main Line ends and meets the Staffordshire & Worcestershire Canal on the outskirts of Wolverhampton. Turning right from the bottom lock, there is a half-mile journey along the Staffordshire & Worcestershire Canal to Autherley Junction, which marks the beginning of the Shropshire Union Canal. When it opened in 1835, most of the traffic that had previously used the Staffordshire & Worcestershire Canal to travel northwards changed to using the new Birmingham & Liverpool Junction Canal. To compensate for the loss of revenue, the Staffordshire & Worcestershire Canal Company imposed a high toll that boats had to pay to use just half a mile of canal. Today's boaters no longer face this imposition so the journey begins at the stop lock at Autherley Junction. The stop lock is only 6 inches deep and was built to protect one canal company's water supply from leaking into the other.

The working boatman called Autherley Junction 'Cut End'. In those days there was a toll office, stables and

Avenue Bridge on the
Chillington Estate.

The spectacular Cowley Cutting.

workshops in front of an elegant junction bridge. The bridge remains and so do many of the original buildings, which are now used by a boatyard and hire fleet. The outlying suburbia of Wolverhampton is soon left behind as the Shropshire Union Canal heads out into the countryside with only the temporary intrusion of the M54 motorway to disturb the peace.

The first notable structure on the canal is the beautiful balustraded Avenue Bridge. Here the canal passes through the Chillington Estate, whose owner insisted the canal builders construct an ornamental bridge to complement the rest of his estate and its gardens, which were landscaped by Capability Brown.

Next comes Brewood (pronounced 'Brood'), a pleasant village with narrow streets and a number of Georgian buildings. The canal at Brewood is situated in a wooded cutting that opens out on to an embankment and then crosses Stretton Aqueduct. Telford's cast-iron aqueduct spans the A5 trunk road (also built by Telford).

Two miles of open countryside leads to Wheaton Aston where there is a waterside pub, boating facilities and a solitary lock. This is in fact the only lock along 25 miles of canal – a tribute to Telford's engineering. Now follow five miles of isolated waterway where the only link with civilisation is the occasional road bridge carrying a country lane. A series of shallow cuttings takes us to Cowley Cutting, one of the deepest and most spectacular on the entire canal; just consider that this immense cutting and the ones that follow were dug by muscle-power long before mechanical excavators had been invented. The men, known as 'navvies', had to move thousands of tons of rock and earth with picks and shovels, then carry it with wheelbarrows until they reached a flat place where horse-power could take over the work. Cowley Cutting is followed by the rock-lined Cowley Tunnel. Beyond the tunnel is the village of Gnosall, with shops and two canalside pubs (one of them, The Boat Inn, was originally built as a horse staging post for the canal).

Gnosall to Market Drayton

After Gnosall comes the Shelmore Embankment. This huge embankment repeatedly collapsed during construction, giving the canal builders a major problem. It was the last piece of this canal to be completed, in 1835, by which time Telford was dead and William Cubitt had to finish the work. Today, the thickly wooded Shelmore Embankment is a delightful place to be, especially in the springtime when it's alive with birdsong.

Shelmore is immediately followed by Norbury Junction, which has a maintenance yard, canal offices, boatyard, pub and cafe. Norbury was once the junction for a network of canals stretching as far as Shrewsbury and the River Severn. Looking from the junction, the first section of the Newport Arm is now used for moorings and the original top lock is now a dry dock for a boatyard. Most of these waterways are derelict and in many cases filled in, but some interesting relics

Waterway Recovery Group

The Waterway Recovery Group (WRG) is a group of dedicated volunteers who give up their weekends and holidays to work with canal societies all over the country, helping to restore derelict waterways back to navigation. The work usually involves using a pick or a shovel (or these days maybe a JCB) to dig out muddy canals, clear overgrown banks and restore lock chambers. This has given rise to the soubriquet 'Dirty Weekenders' which aptly describes these hard-working volunteers. Many develop skills such as bricklaying and driving mechanical diggers and excavators. Although originally independent, WRG is now affiliated to the Inland Waterways Association. WRG activities take place whatever the weather throughout the year.

LEFT **WRG volunteers working on a disused lock.**

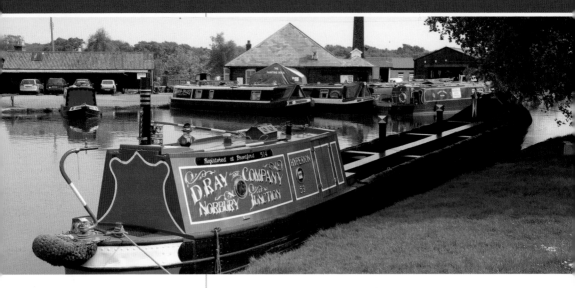

Chocolate Charlie

One of Cadbury's canal boat skippers was Charlie Atkins. Born in 1902, after 14 years' service carrying for Cadburys he became known throughout the waterways as 'Chocolate Charlie'. It is said that children would wait for him by the Birmingham Canal Main Line, hoping to receive a generous handful of chocolate crumb from his cargo as a reward for helping him pass through the locks. The canal boat service ended in 1962 in favour of faster road transport. Chocolate Charlie died in 1981. The Knighton factory is still in production, making powders that are used in custard, jelly and chocolate drinks.

still remain, such as the Longdon-on-Tern Aqueduct near Telford. The Newport Arm of the Shrewsbury Canal that once connected to the Shropshire Union main line at Norbury Junction is currently under restoration with support from Waterway Recovery Group volunteers.

After Norbury there are 11 miles of remote countryside with three canalside pubs and little else. This rural isolation is what makes the Shropshire Union Canal so popular with boaters who want to get away from the trials of modern life. Stocking up with provisions at Gnosall is vital because villages are few and far between and none are actually next to the canal, so it's a long walk to the nearest shop.

Grub Street Cutting is the first place of interest after leaving Norbury. This beautiful wooded cutting is spanned by High Bridge with its double arch supporting a now defunct telegraph pole. Next to Bridge 42 is an isolated canalside pub by a lane that eventually leads to the village of High Offley. After the cutting comes the next embankment at Shebdon. This is as impressive as its predecessors and also has a canalside pub by a minor road that runs under the canal. At the northern end of Shebdon Embankment is Cadbury's Knighton factory, opened over 100 years ago to produce chocolate crumb using milk from neighbouring farms. This chocolate crumb was the basic ingredient for making milk chocolate and it was sent to Cadbury's Bournville factory by their own fleet of canal boats.

Another three miles of open countryside lead to Goldstone Wharf, where there is another canalside pub. Then follows the deep, forested Woodseaves Cutting, spanned by a number of elegant tall bridges. The cutting is very narrow in places and boats should be careful when passing each other.

Woodseaves Cutting ends at Tyrley Wharf. There is a group of houses and the first of five locks on the Tyrley Flight; the first locks since the isolated one at Wheaton Aston 17 miles away. Tyrley Locks drop the canal into the red sandstone Tyrley Cutting, where overhanging trees transform it into a green tunnel.

After Tyrley, the canal enters the busy Betton Mill Wharf at Market Drayton with its boatyard, boating facilities, moorings and fine old warehouses.

The canal keeps its distance from the town centre, so reaching it involves a longish walk or a bus ride. Market Drayton was the birthplace in 1725 of Robert Clive, better known as 'Clive of India'. As a youth he had a reputation for being unruly and on one occasion climbed the church tower and stood on the gargoyles. His school, which stands next to the 14th-century church, has a desk carved with his initials.

ABOVE **Tyrley Locks.**

OPPOSITE **Norbury Junction.**

BELOW **Betton Mill Wharf at Market Drayton.**

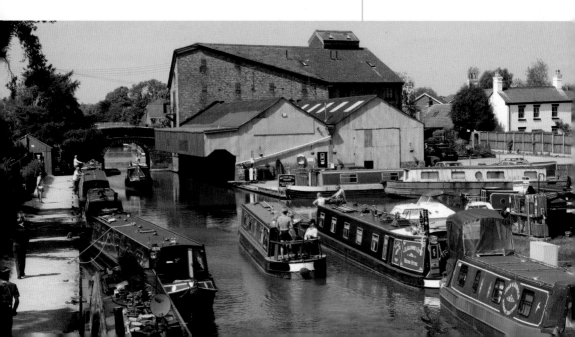

Market Drayton to Middlewich

Beyond Market Drayton, the canal returns to open and remote farming countryside. At Betton Wood there is a short cutting that is reputed to be the home of a shrieking ghost. The working boatmen were convinced that this was true and would never stop here.

Soon after this, there are five more locks to negotiate at Adderley. The village is half a mile from the canal and best reached from the bridge beyond the top lock.

Adderley Locks are just a warm-up for the 15 locks that follow on the Audlem Lock Flight. However, they're pleasantly situated, with fine views over the surrounding countryside, so there's something to look at while you work.

The village of Audlem is close to the bottom four locks, where there are two excellent waterside pubs, and a mill converted into a craft centre and bookshop. Shops and a general store are close to the canal, which makes Audlem a good place for boaters to stock up on essential goods.

Hack Green, three miles beyond Audlem, has two locks, and is the location of the 'Secret Nuclear Bunker'. Judging by the signs on the road and another by the canal, the 'secret' bunker is no longer so clandestine. Originally built as a headquarters for regional government in case of a nuclear attack, it opened as a museum with a Cold War theme in 1998 and is now open daily to the public during the summer months and on weekends during the winter.

A long embankment carries the canal into Nantwich, where it crosses a busy road on an aqueduct next to Nantwich Basin. Reached by making a sharp left turn at the junction with the Chester Canal, Nantwich Basin was the former terminus of the Chester Canal. Today it is home to the Nantwich Canal Centre, which has a boatyard, moorings, chandlery and cafe. Nantwich has some fine old buildings as well as numerous shops, pubs and restaurants.

TOP **Audlem Locks.**

ABOVE **The Shroppie Fly pub and crane at Audlem Locks.**

LEFT ABOVE **The 100-year-old narrowboat** Saturn **at Adderley Locks.** Saturn **is the last Shropshire Union Canal fly-boat, originally built to travel non-stop, day and night, carrying perishable goods.**

LEFT **Sign for the Secret Nuclear Bunker at Hack Green.**

Maureen Shaw

Wardle Lock was the home of former working boat woman Maureen Shaw. Maureen was abandoned by her mother when still a baby, and given away to a couple who were working boat people and who brought her up as their own daughter. She worked on their boat, usually helping with the horse until their boat became motorised. Later she married boatman John Shaw who worked for Fellows, Morton & Clayton Ltd. Together they carried varied cargoes such as sugar, flour and metal tubes on his boat. After she retired, Maureen would still cheerfully help boaters through her lock. Although she never learned to read or write, in later life Maureen gave lucid talks about her life as a working boat woman, including an interview on national radio. After her death in 2012, a plaque was erected in her memory at Wardle Lock.

RIGHT **Maureen Shaw at Wardle Lock in 1998.**

The junction bridge marks the end of the original Birmingham & Liverpool Junction Canal. We continue along to Hurleston, which is the junction with the Chester Canal and the Llangollen Canal. Boats heading for Llangollen have to negotiate a flight of locks at Hurleston and there are often queues of craft waiting to enter the bottom lock.

Barbridge Junction is a mile beyond Hurleston, and has a marina, a boatyard and two pubs with restaurants next to the canal and a busy main road. This is where we leave the Shropshire Union Main Line and turn right for Middlewich.

The Middlewich Branch is ten miles long and has four locks. A large marina by Cholmondeston Lock has a tea room as well as boating facilities. There is another marina at Church Minshull, and the village has a pub and restaurant. The Middlewich Branch is very peaceful and entirely rural, passing through remote farming countryside with occasional

The Middlewich Branch.

areas of woodland. At times there are wide views across the Weaver Valley towards lakes called the Winsford Flashes.

Eventually the canal reaches Middlewich and its junction with the Trent & Mersey Canal. The final lock on the Middlewich Branch is Wardle Lock.

The Anderton
Boat Lift.

Chapter 8

TRENT & MERSEY CANAL

NORTH SECTION

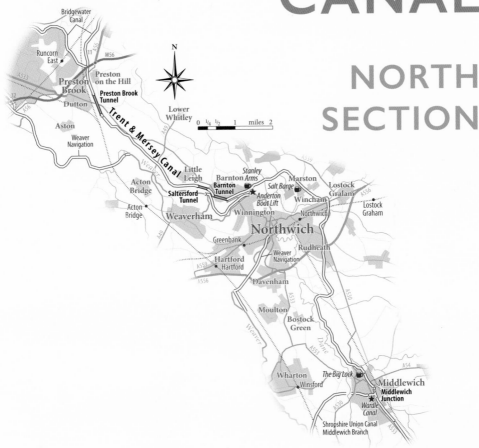

Following the success of the Bridgewater Canal in Manchester, its engineer James Brindley planned to build a network of canals to connect the rivers Trent, Mersey, Severn and Thames. Originally known as the Grand Trunk Canal, the Trent & Mersey Canal was financed by Josiah Wedgwood and other pottery owners in Stoke-on-Trent. These potters were keen to bring in raw materials more efficiently, and safely transport their delicate finished produce that had until then been carried by packhorses on rutted roads. The 17-mile-long northern section between Preston Brook and Middlewich was also designed as a broad canal for the use of salt barges.

TRENT & MERSEY CANAL
NORTH SECTION

Construction of the 93-mile-long Trent & Mersey Canal began in 1766 but tunnelling problems at Harecastle delayed the opening until 1777, by which time Brindley had died and therefore never saw the completion of his dream navigation. Today, the Trent & Mersey Canal is one of England's most popular cruising waterways and in Chapter 14 of this journey we will also be travelling on the eastern section, between Shardlow and Fradley Junction.

View from the junction of the Trent & Mersey Canal at Middlewich.

Middlewich to Anderton

The journey begins at the Wardle Canal, which at 155 feet is the shortest canal in Britain. It connects Wardle Lock (at the end of the Shropshire Union's Middlewich Arm) to the junction, and was built by the Trent Navigation Company as a controlling link between them and the Shropshire Union. A worn plaque on the bridge states 'Wardle Canal 1829'.

Middlewich was founded by the Romans, who named it Salinae because of its salt deposits. The suffix 'wich' has Old English origins and again refers to salt towns, such as Northwich and Nantwich. Salt is still manufactured in the town but on a much smaller scale than a hundred years ago, when the canal was lined by salt works with forests of smoking chimneys.

The Kings Lock and pub at Middlewich.

Leaving the junction you turn left, passing a number of boatyards to reach three narrow-gauge locks. The next lock, aptly called Middlewich Big Lock, was built as a wide lock to enable salt barges working between Middlewich and Preston Brook to pass. The attendant pub is also known as The Big Lock Pub and Restaurant and is particularly busy during the folk and boat festival that takes place every summer by the canal in the town.

Croxton Aqueduct crosses the River Dane just outside Middlewich. It was damaged by flooding in the 1930s and rebuilt with a very narrow channel, so there is only room for one boat to cross at a time.

After the aqueduct, the canal follows the River Dane Valley. This delightful three-mile-long section of woodland and flashes caused by mining subsidence is a paradise for waterfowl. Some of the lagoons were used as a dumping ground for abandoned canal boats, but in recent years most of them have been raised and removed. Nevertheless, boaters

TOP LEFT **Croxton Aqueduct.**

BOTTOM LEFT **Middlewich Big Lock.**

The Salt Barge pub opposite the Lion Salt Works at Marston.

are warned not to stray into these areas as the odd sunken vessel may still lurk beneath the waters.

A boatyard by Bridge 182 marks the end of the lovely Dane Valley section and heralds an industrial area on the outskirts of Northwich.

The Lion Salt Works at Marston was the last factory in Britain to use the open-pan process to evaporate brine. It closed in 1986 and later re-opened as a working salt museum. Marston's fame for its salt mines was highlighted by a visit from the Tsar of Russia in 1844, when he was guest of honour at a banquet hosted by the Royal Society in the caverns 300 feet below the surface. The canal, which played a major role in transporting salt from Marston, suffered a collapse through subsidence at the beginning of the 20th century and a new section of canal had to be cut.

The 200-acre Marbury Country Park near Marston is also worth visiting. Access to the park's visitor centre is from the canal by Bridge 196. After this comes Anderton Marina, with all boating facilities and a restaurant. The marina is followed by the famous Anderton Boat Lift.

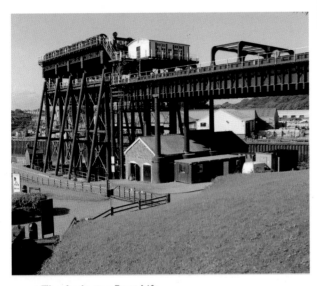

ABOVE **The Anderton Boat Lift.**

The Anderton Boat Lift

The Anderton Boat Lift was built in 1875 to connect the Trent & Mersey Canal to the River Weaver Navigation 50 feet below. It was designed by Edward Leader Williams, who was later responsible for building the Manchester Ship Canal. The lift has a frame that holds two water-filled tanks. These tanks were originally supported on hydraulic rams, so that as one tank rose, the other descended. Electricity replaced steam in 1903 and counterbalanced weights replaced the hydraulic system in 1908. In more recent times the lift suffered severe corrosion because of chemical pollution from nearby works and in 1983 it had to be closed for safety reasons. Restored and reopened in 2002, it now has a visitor centre with information on its history. A trip boat also gives visitors the opportunity of experiencing the lift at first hand. The Anderton Lift has now become one of the most popular tourist attractions in north-west England.

OPPOSITE Industrial section at Wincham near Northwich.

Anderton to Preston Brook Tunnel

Boating on an elevated section above the Weaver Valley, near Acton Bridge.

Leaving Anderton, the canal and River Weaver are close companions for several miles. At first there is heavy industry between the two waterways before the river bends away from the canal for a short while. The canal then passes through

two short tunnels in quick succession. Barnton Tunnel is 572 yards long and Saltersford is 424 yards long, and neither are wide enough for two boats to pass inside. They have no towpaths so in each case walkers have to take a stroll over the top, following the path once used by the working boat horses. The River Weaver is very close to the tunnel at Saltersford and a steep path takes you down to Saltersford Lock, which makes a pleasant route for walkers.

After Saltersford Tunnel, the canal continues through woodland with views across the Weaver Valley. At the boatyard by Acton Bridge, consider a short walk down the road to see the impressive Acton Swing Bridge over the River Weaver. An adjacent pub and restaurant completes a worthwhile diversion.

After Acton Bridge, the two waterways part company and the Trent & Mersey Canal follows a mostly wooded two-mile course to Preston Brook Tunnel, which marks the end of the 93-mile-long canal. Just before the tunnel's entrance at Dutton there is a dry dock and a stop lock. The 1,239-yard-long tunnel has no towpath so walkers must again follow the hoofprints of the long-dead working boat horses over the top.

practical information

Distance: Middlewich to Preston Brook is 17 miles with 5 locks and 3 tunnels.

Boaters: Preston Brook is a long tunnel, so for northbound boats access to the tunnel is restricted to entry from on the hour to ten minutes past the hour. Saltersford and Barnton Tunnels are shorter in length but both have restricted entry times.

Walkers: None of the tunnels has a towpath so walkers must take the footpath over the top.

Places of interest: The Anderton Boat Lift and the Wardle Canal at Middlewich, which is the shortest canal in Britain.

Key pubs: Stanley Arms at Anderton; Salt Barge at Marston; and The Big Lock at Middlewich.

Preston Brook Tunnel.

Chapter 9

BRIDGEWATER
CANAL

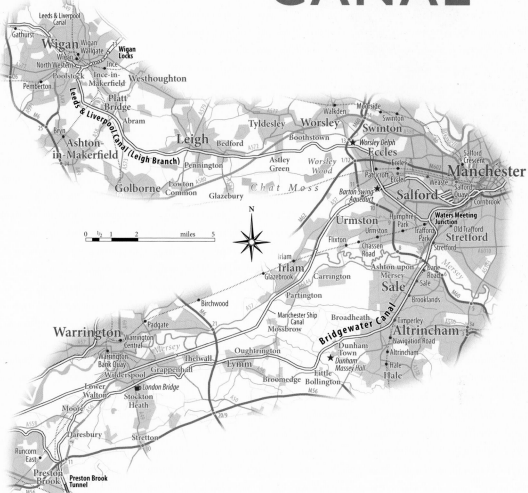

The Bridgewater Canal between Worsley and Manchester opened in 1765, making it the oldest canal in Britain still in regular use. Today, most of the canal passes through Manchester and its suburbs, making it a refuge for local people and a fascinating cruising waterway for visiting boaters. One or two sections have a rural aspect, in particular between Lymm and Sale and again west of Worsley, otherwise the canal is flanked by industry and housing.

**Bridgewater Canal near
Preston Brook Tunnel.**

The canal was planned by Francis Egerton, 3rd Duke of Bridgewater, as an economical method of transporting coal from his Worsley mines to Manchester. Earlier attempts to carry coal by road proved useless as the roads were in bad condition and half a ton was the maximum load a horse was capable of pulling. Put the same horse in front of a barge, however, and it could move 30 tons with little effort.

As a young man on his Grand Tour of Europe, the Duke had seen canal transport in action on the Canal du Midi in France. The Duke's agent John Gilbert devised a scheme whereby natural water accumulation in the mines was turned into a system of underground canals that fed to the surface. From there, Gilbert and pioneering canal engineer James Brindley built their canal to Manchester.

One problem they faced was how to cross the River Irwell, and to solve this Brindley built his aqueduct at Barton, known at the time as 'the canal in the air'. From here to Manchester the canal was completed on the same contour level, avoiding the construction of any locks. An extension of the canal between Stretford and Runcorn was completed in 1772. This branch remained on the level all the way to Runcorn, where a flight of ten locks connected it to the River Mersey. Later a short arm linked to the Trent & Mersey Canal at Preston Brook Tunnel, which is where we continue our journey. Boats holding a Canal & River Trust licence can cruise on the Bridgewater Canal for seven days free of charge.

Preston Brook to Sale

Leaving the Trent & Mersey Canal inside Preston Brook Tunnel, you emerge into the Bridgewater Canal on the other side. Preston Brook was once a busy transhipment place where wide Mersey flat boats transferred cargoes to narrowboats. The canal was lined with warehouses, most of which have now either been demolished or converted into housing. Today there is a lot of moorings and a boatyard with a hire fleet.

The junction with the main line and the Runcorn Arm is just beyond the M56 motorway viaduct. The Runcorn Arm is now a dead-end as the ten locks down to the Mersey are derelict. The five-mile-long arm finishes in Runcorn town centre and is worth a diversion. Norton Priory Museum & Gardens can be reached from Bridge 75 on the Runcorn Arm, and Preston Brook Marina is close to the junction.

Back on the main line, the canal continues in a north-easterly direction to Daresbury, where a prominent tower

ABOVE **Waterloo Bridge at Runcorn.**

BELOW **A busy day at a Preston Brook boatyard.**

The Bridgewater Canal at Lymm. marks the site of the Daresbury Laboratory, a renowned science institute. Daresbury is also famous for being the birthplace of Lewis Carroll, and the local church has a Lewis Carroll window and a visitor centre.

The canal passes through the village of Moore to Walton Hall, which is hidden from the waterway by trees and rhododendrons. Walton Hall has beautiful gardens, a cafe and a children's zoo. Next comes Stockton Heath, a suburb of Warrington. The Manchester Ship Canal is just a short walk down the hill from The London Bridge pub.

Grappenhall comes next, with a 16th-century church, a cobbled street, village stocks, and a couple of good pubs. After Grappenhall, the canal passes beneath the towering Thelwall Viaduct that carries the M6 motorway over the Manchester Ship Canal and River Mersey. Take time to visit the charming town of Lymm, which has a canalside market every Thursday and plenty of moorings for visiting boats.

After Lymm, the canal passes through three miles of open countryside with a group of boatyards, a marina and a pub.

For walkers on the opposite side of the canal (there's no crossing point for half a mile), the pub offers a ferry service.

Dunham Massey Hall, near the village of Dunham Town, dates back to 1616 and was rebuilt in Georgian times. It is now owned by the National Trust. The moated house is open to the public, and boasts a collection of Huguenot silver and some fine paintings. It also has a large deer park.

Beyond Dunham it is goodbye to the countryside as Oldfield Brow marks the approach to Sale and Greater Manchester. Oldfield Quay has a marina, followed at Broadheath by an extraordinary group of apartment buildings designed to look like ocean liners, which lean over the canal. Compare these startling examples of modern architecture with the adjacent canal warehouses and the nearby Linotype building, which was built in 1897.

Dunham Massey Hall.

The canal in the centre of Sale.

The canal takes a straight line through Sale, with its waterside pubs and access to the town centre at Sale Bridge. The Waterside Arts Centre and Robert Bolt Theatre are also close to Sale Bridge. Sale railway station, near the canal, is on the Metrolink rail service that provides direct access to central Manchester. Leaving Sale, the canal passes beneath the M60 motorway, which runs by the Sale Water Park and the River Mersey.

Sale to Worsley

At Stretford the canal passes a boatyard and cruising club moorings and on to Waters Meeting junction. Here the canal splits, with the Manchester line travelling on to the city centre, via Salford Quays and Manchester United's Old Trafford football stadium. Instead, we follow the Leigh Branch through Trafford Park, a huge industrial estate that includes Courtaulds chemical manufacturing company and the Kellogg's factory, which once used the canal for transportation. Today, much of the industrial landscape is softened by lines of trees on both sides of the water. The Trafford Shopping Centre is close to Bridge 46.

Now we arrive at the remarkable Barton Swing Aqueduct, which was built in 1894, replacing Brindley's 130-year-old original structure. The construction of the Manchester Ship Canal meant that Brindley's aqueduct was too short and too low to allow ships to pass beneath it on their way to

The Barton Swing Aqueduct in the closed position.

The Duke of Bridgewater's mines

Within the Duke of Bridgewater's mines at Worsley there were around 46 miles of subterranean waterways on different levels, and specially designed boats called 'starvationers' carried coal from the coalface to the surface. Various methods of transport were used, including an inclined plane and shafts with vertical lifts. Following the construction of his canal to take the coal on to Manchester, the Duke of Bridgewater became known as 'The Father of Inland Navigation'. This appellation can be seen inscribed on the monument at his Ashridge Estate near Tring in Hertfordshire.

This magnificent half-timbered Packet House was once the terminus for a passenger boat service between Worsley and Manchester. The entrance to the Duke's mines can be seen behind the bridge on the right of the picture.

Today, all you can see of the entrance to the Duke's mines is a boarded-up tunnel with the water around it stained orange from seepages within the mine. This colour stains the canal for some distance around Worsley. Although the Worsley mines closed a long time ago, there were still regular inspections by the coal authorities because other working collieries in the area used them for drainage and ventilation. All the mines finally closed in 1968.

Manchester's docks. Edward Leader Williams, who engineered the Ship Canal, designed an aqueduct that could swing away when a ship came along. When a ship is expected, gates are closed to seal the Bridgewater Canal at each end and then the aqueduct swings open until it is at a right angle to the Ship Canal. The closure of Manchester's docks has reduced the frequency of passing ships, so boaters using the aqueduct should be able to cross without having to wait. Walkers cannot cross the aqueduct so must use the adjacent Barton Road Bridge and rejoin the canal at the other side.

The canal then continues through Patricroft to Monton, which has an incongruous lighthouse folly opposite the Barge Inn at Bridge 50. A sharp bend leads to Worsley, where the canal age began in 1761 with the building of the Bridgewater Canal.

The Barton Swing Aqueduct in the open position, allowing a coaster to pass through.

Worsley to Leigh

Leaving Worsley beneath a mass of motorway ring roads, the canal enters an area of open countryside with occasional sections of woodland on the northern fringe of Chat Moss. There was once a system of canals here serving the industries of Chat Moss, but they were abandoned and filled in long ago. At Boothstown Bridge there is a boatyard and a pub, but little else until you reach Astley Green.

The Astley Green Colliery Museum opened in 1970, following the closure of the pit. Its engine house and headgear are the only remaining examples left on the Lancashire coalfield. It has a collection of 28 colliery locomotives and its 98-feet-high headgear (the stocks and

Pithead winding gear at Astley Green Colliery Museum.

wheels that lifted men, materials and coal up and down the shafts) can be seen for miles around.

Coal gives way to cotton as the canal enters Leigh. The pits may have gone but there is still plenty of evidence of cotton mills in the area. Cotton imported through the Port of Liverpool turned towns such as Leigh and Wigan into cotton-spinning areas, made prosperous by the transport potential of the Leeds & Liverpool Canal and Bridgewater Canal. Bedford, on the outskirts of Leigh, has the magnificent six-storey Butts Mill, followed by another at Mather Lane, both next to the canal. In 1910, Leigh employed nearly 7,000 people in the cotton industry. Many of the old mills have been demolished and in some places new apartment blocks have been designed to look like the mills they replaced.

Leigh Bridge is the best stopping place for visiting the town centre, and it also marks the point where the Bridgewater Canal gives way to the Leigh Branch of the Leeds & Liverpool Canal.

ABOVE **Leigh Bridge, where the Bridgewater Canal becomes the Leeds & Liverpool Canal.**

BELOW **Mather Lane Mill at Leigh.**

Leigh to Wigan

The Leigh Branch of the Leeds & Liverpool Canal opened in 1820, connecting to the Bridgewater Canal and thereby creating an important water artery from Wigan to the south. The canal is seven miles long and has two locks at Wigan, which are the only locks we'll encounter in the 42 miles between Preston Brook and Wigan.

Beyond Leigh the canal passes through countryside once dominated by coal mining. The last pit in the area was Bickershaw Colliery, which closed in 1992. It was situated next to the canal at Plank Lane and used water transport to carry coal to power stations at Wigan. Bickershaw had a

Plank Lane Lift Bridge.

Cruising on Leigh Branch.

renowned colliery brass band that won several prizes in national and regional competitions. Nothing remains of the colliery now and some of the area next to Plank Lane Lift Bridge has become a marina. Plank Lane Lift Bridge is boater-operated, but be aware that it is closed for rush-hour traffic. On the opposite side is Pennington Flash, a 170-acre lake created by mining subsidence from Bickershaw Colliery, and now a beautiful country park and nature reserve.

Dover Bridge, which has the only waterside pub on the Leigh Branch, is one of the few motor-crossing points on this open section of canal. There were once two locks here but mining subsidence caused the canal to drop and made the locks redundant, so they were removed. In the final two miles before Wigan, the canal passes along a bleak area of wasteland that was once the site of collieries. More flashes caused by mining subsidence relieve the flat landscape and provide homes to a variety of birdlife. Then come the two locks at Poolstock. The canal joins the main line of the Leeds & Liverpool Canal below the locks at a point once dominated by the Westwood Power Station, which is sadly no more and has been replaced by offices.

practical information

Distance: Preston Brook to Wigan is 42 miles with just 2 locks at Wigan.

Boaters: Plank Lane Lift Bridge is manned by a bridge keeper but can be self operated when he is not on duty.

Walkers: The towpath is continuous and in good condition throughout.

Places of interest: Worsley Delph – where the canal age began; Dunham Massey Hall; and the Barton Swing Aqueduct.

Key pubs: London Bridge at Stockton Heath. A lot of pubs have closed in this area.

Daisyfield Mill at Blackburn.

Chapter 10

LEEDS & LIVERPOOL
CANAL

The Leeds & Liverpool Canal is the longest man-made waterway in Britain and is an integral part of an inland route between the Irish Sea and the North Sea. Work began on the 127-mile-long canal in 1770 and it took 46 years to complete. It finally opened in 1816, making it the first of the three trans-Pennine canals to be started but the last to be completed. The complex route over the Pennine hills, along with a total of 91 locks, raised the building costs and presented severe financial problems to the canal company.

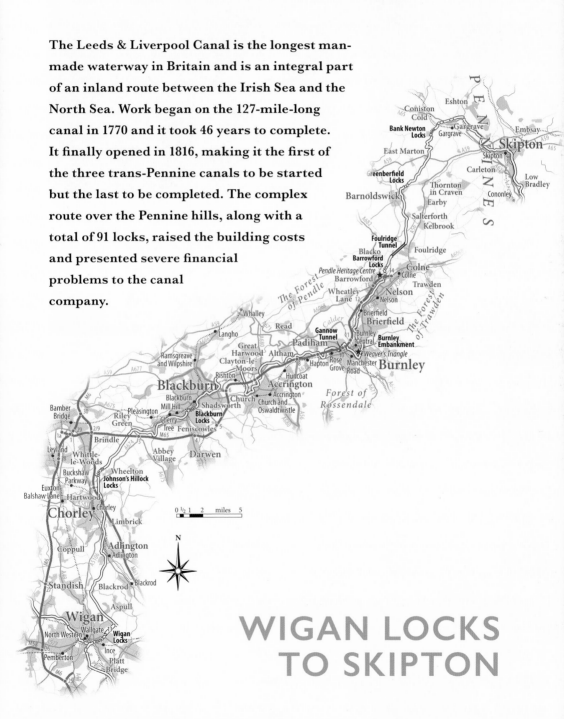

WIGAN LOCKS
TO SKIPTON

Blackburn Waterside sign.

The fact that the Leeds & Liverpool Canal linked the Port of Liverpool with the industrial towns of Burnley, Blackburn, Nelson, Wigan and Leeds made the canal an important commercial artery. Coal, cotton, wool, grain, sugar and machinery were all key commodities carried on its waters in its heyday, which lasted until the late 1950s. When commercial carrying ended, its neighbours (the Rochdale Canal and the Huddersfield Canal) were closed and abandoned, but the Leeds & Liverpool Canal stayed open. Its winding course over the Pennine moorland, together with its journey through old Lancashire cotton-mill towns and dramatic engineering features such as the Bingley Five-rise Locks staircase, have made the Leeds & Liverpool Canal a popular cruising waterway. Boaters should be aware that all locks between Wigan and Leeds are 60 feet long and therefore cannot accommodate a full-length narrowboat.

Wigan to Chorley

The two locks at the end of the Leigh Branch are the first to be encountered since Middlewich, almost 60 miles away. At Wigan, the hard work begins with 21 locks to negotiate in two miles. Before turning right into the first lock, boaters and walkers should take some time to visit the Wigan Pier area. Turn left and very soon you will see the impressive Trencherfield Mill. Built in 1907, this former cotton mill's main attraction is the world's largest mill steam engine. The engine has been restored to full working order, and the rest of the mill converted to other purposes. The nearby pub at Wigan Pier was once a cotton warehouse, and now calls itself The Orwell. The Wigan Pier in question was a cast-iron tippler at a coal staithe, and can be seen on the opposite side of the canal from the pub. The name Wigan Pier was first

Wigan Locks.

Leeds & Liverpool Canal at Heath Charnock near Chorley.

made famous as a joke by comedian George Formby Sr, and was then used in the title of a book by George Orwell.

Back at the locks you begin a climb of about 200 feet, with views of Wigan gradually opening up behind you. The surroundings are green and mostly rather agreeable, but it wasn't always like this. Orwell's *The Road to Wigan Pier* describes the lock environs as a lunar landscape of slag heaps backed by factory chimneys belching out plumes of smoke. It was a world where vegetation had been banished, leaving behind smoke, mud and foul water. There was a colliery by the canal at Rose Bridge and further on a huge ironworks dominated the skyline with blast furnaces, coke ovens and high smoking chimneys. Some of the former slag heaps have been grassed over and now offer panoramic views of the town and surrounding countryside. As you reach the top of the flight, there is the welcoming sight of a pub next to the top lock.

Beyond the top lock there is a sharp left turn leading to a section of canal once shared by the Leeds & Liverpool Canal and Lancaster Canal. Originally built by the Lancaster Canal, it was joined by the Leeds & Liverpool Canal at Johnson's Hillock Locks and ran to Wigan Top Lock. It was intended to continue the Lancaster Canal to Westhoughton, and from there possibly to connect to the Bridgewater Canal at Worsley. However, lack of finances brought the scheme to a halt at Monk Hall Bridge by Wigan Top Lock and the extension was never built.

Leaving Wigan behind, the canal enters a section of wooded waterway with little in the way of habitation for four miles. Haigh Hall Country Park is worth a visit, offering a mansion, gardens, 250 acres of parkland and a golf course. A little further on there is a canalside pub at Red Rock and another golf course in the grounds of Arley Hall. Adlington's White Bear Marina and cafe is followed by a boatyard with a hire fleet at Heath Charnock. Woodland screens the road and railway that follow the canal in this section, but you glimpse occasional views of the tower on Rivington Pike, which stands at 1,200 feet on top of moorland to the east.

The canal keeps to the eastern edge of Chorley, where it passes the Botany Bay Village. Here a former five-storey mill building sandwiched between the canal and the M61 motorway has been converted to a lively shopping centre. Also not to be missed is the renowned Frederick's Ice Cream Parlour near Bridge 73 at Heath Charnock, on the southern edge of Chorley.

Botany Bay Mill Shopping Centre at Chorley.

Chorley to Blackburn

The entrance to the Walton Summit Branch of the Lancaster Canal can be seen at the foot of the seven locks at Johnson's Hillock. The original intention of the Lancaster Canal Company was to build an aqueduct over the River Ribble to connect to Preston, but as often happens a lack of finances led to the compromise of a tramroad on a trestle bridge. The line was opened in 1803, but was never a success and was abandoned in 1880. The beautifully situated flight of locks at Johnson's Hillock has a pub and a boatyard at the top lock.

Another lovely wooded section leads to Withnell Fold, where there once stood a paper mill that printed the paper for bank notes. Withnell Fold was a model village built by the mill owners for its workers. It has a cobbled street and a village green, but the mill has gone and has been replaced by light industrial units. Withnell Fold also has a nature reserve created from a series of old filter beds.

Johnson's Hillock Locks.

After Withnell Fold there are several miles of hills and open countryside. The Boatyard Inn at Riley Green is a useful stopping point, and was built on the site of an old boatbuilding yard. The canal then bends south to Feniscowles, where there were more paper mills, before entering the town of Blackburn through a suburb with the charming name of Cherry Tree.

The canal arrives in Blackburn on an embankment, allowing extensive views across the town to its cathedral, a brewery and Ewood Park, home of Blackburn Rovers Football Club. An aqueduct is followed by six locks that raise the canal to the canopied Eanam Wharf, whose depot was once the focal point of the town's canal activity. The building is now a business development centre with a pub appropriately called The Depot. Eanam Wharf has a canal visitor centre and is the best place for boaters to stock up with provisions and visit the town centre. The Blackburn Canal Festival is an annual three-day event in July.

Notable waterside buildings include Daisyfield Mill, the largest surviving corn mill in the Blackburn area, which is now occupied by a variety of businesses. At the edge of Blackburn, a retail park has replaced Whitebirk Power Station, which was the location for the last regular coal traffic on this section of canal.

Eanam Wharf, Blackburn.

Blackburn textile industry

Blackburn once ranked as one of Britain's leading textile-producing towns, and the canal played a vital role in its prosperity, supplying Blackburn's mills with imported raw cotton and coal and carrying away the finished produce. The town's skyline was adorned with hundreds of mill and factory chimneys – one by the canal was reputed to be the tallest in England. By the middle of the 20th century the textile industry was in decline, and most of these giants have since been demolished, although a few still remain.

Blackburn to Burnley

The canal finally leaves Blackburn behind and heads out through hilly countryside to Rishton. It then bends to the south and twists and turns in a series of exaggerated loops through Church to Clayton-le-Moors. At Church, which marks the halfway point on the canal between Leeds and Liverpool, look out for the so-called Fairy Caves – secluded ancient monuments connected to the former Aspen Coke Ovens. This was once an important coal-mining area, but the mines have all gone. Church also has the first of the swing bridges that will soon become all too familiar to boaters travelling in an easterly direction. After Clayton-le-Moors,

Most of the buildings in Burnley shown in this photo, taken in the 1970s, have since been demolished.

the M65 motorway becomes a noisy neighbour all the way to Burnley. Clayton was the site of Moorfield Colliery, where 69 miners were killed in an underground explosion in 1883. Comedian Eric Morecambe worked in the pit as a Bevin Boy during the Second World War.

Despite the proximity of the motorway, the canal takes a pleasant winding course through mostly open countryside with views of hills and moorland on both sides of the waterway. On a clear day, Pendle Hill can be seen to the north and the Forest of Rossendale to the south. Hapton has a pub, a general store and a boatyard with overnight mooring. Then, after two more miles, Rose Grove heralds the outskirts of Burnley. Rose Grove Wharf has full facilities for boaters plus shops, a fish and chip shop and a railway station whose engine shed was one of the last to house steam locomotives on British railways.

The canal's entry into Burnley is by the 559-yard-long Gannow Tunnel. There is no towpath so walkers must go over the top, which at one point involves passing through a

A cantilevered weaver's warehouse at Burnley Wharf which also has a pub and the Weaver's Triangle Visitor Centre.

Burnley Embankment is one of the 'Seven Wonders of the Waterways'.

pedestrian underpass beneath the motorway. At the other end the canal crosses over the motorway on a new aqueduct before entering what is known as the 'Weaver's Triangle', which was a collection of 19th-century corn mills and associated buildings.

Burnley became a textile centre in the early 1700s and by 1910 there were 100,000 power looms working in the town, producing more cloth than anywhere else in the world. The Weaver's Triangle celebrates Burnley's pre-eminence as a textile town, with a canalside visitor centre at Burnley Wharf telling the story of the cotton industry and the canal's role in its success. The surrounding area has waterside weaving sheds, mills and canal warehouses, although the impressive Clock Tower Mill was damaged by fire in 1987 and had to be demolished.

Next comes the three-quarter-mile-long Burnley Embankment, which runs in a dead-straight line 60 feet above the rooftops in the centre of the town. It gives boaters and walkers a panoramic view of the town's streets, Burnley's Turf Moor football stadium and the hills at the back of the town. It carries the canal over a small river and has two aqueducts. The embankment is generally recognised as one of the 'Seven Wonders of the Waterways'.

At the end of the embankment there is a sharp bend at Thompson Park followed by a lovely wooded section.

Burnley to Foulridge

The canal now follows a northerly course for five miles between Burnley and Nelson. There is much evidence of the area's industrial past in the form of old textile mills. Many of these have been converted to new purposes, especially at Brierfield where there are also shops and a railway station close to the canal. On this section of waterway, the east side of the canal is mostly built up, but there are good views of the surrounding hills to the west beyond the motorway.

Nelson is a former cotton-mill town that has lost most of the industry that once made it prosperous. A recent heritage campaign has saved a couple of mills and some Victorian terraced housing from demolition. Radical left-wing politics in the early 20th century led to the town being labelled 'Little Moscow'. This is not a sobriquet that can be used today, as is evidenced by the wide array of ethnic restaurants and shops owned by a large Asian population in the town.

Barrowford Locks.

The canal climbs seven locks at Barrowford, where it immerses itself into the moorland all the way to distant Skipton. Industrial Lancashire is now left behind in Nelson and so is the M65 motorway, which has been a constant companion for 25 miles. A reservoir by the locks supplies water to the canal's summit level.

Before leaving Barrowford Locks, consider taking a walk to the excellent Pendle Heritage Centre in Barrowford village. Here you can visit a museum sited in a 15th-century farmhouse and learn about the notorious Pendle Witches trials in 1612. All this is on offer inside a walled garden in a village where the late Dr Roger Bannister, the first athlete to achieve a 4-minute mile, was born.

Pendle Heritage Centre.

Continuing to Foulridge, we encounter the longest tunnel on the canal. Foulridge Tunnel achieved fame in 1912 when a cow called Buttercup fell into the canal and swam the entire 1,640 yards to the other end, where it was revived with brandy. Today's boaters do not have Buttercup's navigational freedom and must obey a system of traffic lights before entering the tunnel. Once again there is no towpath, so walkers have to pick their way over the top, following the track of an old railway. Foulridge Wharf has a cafe/bistro in an old canal company building. There is also a restored lime kiln and a trip boat.

Foulridge Wharf.

Foulridge to Skipton

The tree-lined canal meanders through a peaceful landscape, with Bridges 149 and 150 at Whitemoor once marking the boundary between Lancashire and Yorkshire, until the boundaries were changed in 1974. The Anchor Inn at Salterforth is a good stopping-off point, and was built on top of an earlier packhorse inn. Rather unusually, it has an array of stalactites and stalagmites in the cellar.

The canal now enters Barnoldswick, which is the highest town on the Leeds & Liverpool Canal, and home to a Rolls Royce engine factory. Barnoldswick has a marina with all facilities for visiting boats, and there is a variety of shops in the town.

The canal's short summit level ends at Greenberfield Locks in a glorious setting amid moorland and hillsides studded with sheep. Here you will see birds such as curlews,

View from the Anchor Inn at Salterforth.

lapwings, skylarks and buzzards, and in the summertime swallows and martins swoop across the surface of the canal searching for insects. This is the landscape that inspired the Brontë sisters, although there's no guarantee you will meet Heathcliff or Catherine around the next bend.

At the top of the three locks at Greenberfield there is a cafe, showers and other boating facilities. Beyond the locks the canal twists and turns, following the contours around the hills. At each turn new vistas open up in every direction, with spectacular views of far horizons. At East Marton, the 16th-century The Cross Keys inn overlooks an unusual double-arched bridge, which carries a main road. There is a restaurant nearby in the village.

A wooded cutting takes the canal away from East Marton and back into the moorland where the waterway's convolutions are even more exaggerated. The towpath on

Greenberfield Top Lock.

TOP **Moorings at East Marton.**

RIGHT **Double-arched bridge at East Marton.**

BELOW **Gargrave** – the most northerly point of our long journey.

this section is part of the 267-mile Pennine Way long-distance footpath so you may see lines of backpacking walkers alongside the canal. Six locks on the Bank Newton Flight lower the canal into the River Aire Valley. These locks are in an idyllic setting, with sweeping views over the hills towards the Yorkshire Dales National Park. The River Aire passes beneath the canal at Priest Holme Aqueduct and then reappears in a picturesque setting by a stone bridge in the centre of Gargrave. There are six locks at Gargrave, but they are well spaced out (unlike the ones at Bank Newton). Do not rush through Gargrave, for there is a lot to see and do, including a visit to the excellent Dalesman Cafe in the village centre. Gargrave also has good pubs and a first-class fish and chippy.

After Holme Bridge Lock, the canal turns to the south-east, following the valley of the River Aire on one side and the border of the Yorkshire Dales National Park on the other, for the three miles to Skipton. Only the presence of the A65 trunk road disturbs the peace of this lovely section of waterway. You will occasionally come across swing bridges, spaced roughly a mile apart. These will become much more frequent in the next part of the journey, after leaving Skipton.

practical information

Distance: Wigan Locks to Skipton is 63 miles with 55 locks.

Boaters: The 55 locks are all 60 feet long and 14.3 feet wide. There are two tunnels, both without a towpath. Boaters will need a Watermate Key for some of the swing bridges.

Walkers: There are railway connections between Gargrave and Skipton and more between Burnley and Nelson, and another between Cherry Tree (Blackburn) and Church (Oswaldtwistle). All these stations are within a short walk from the canal.

Places of interest: Weaver's Triangle at Burnley; Moorland countryside between Barrowford and Skipton; and Pendle Heritage Centre at Barrowford.

Key pubs: There are lots of good waterside pubs throughout this section.

Entering Skipton through a swing bridge.

Chapter 11

Bingley Five Rise Locks.

LEEDS & LIVERPOOL CANAL

SKIPTON TO LEEDS

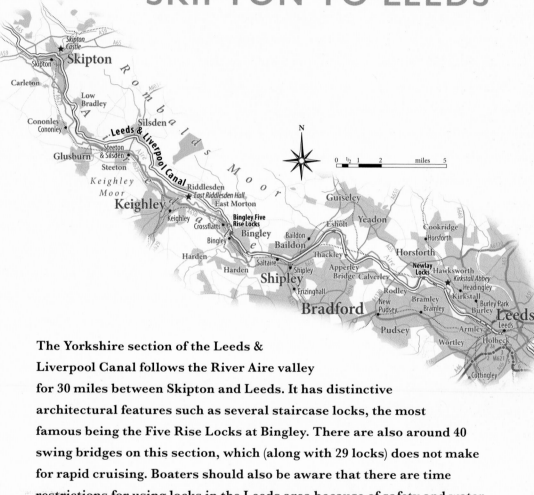

The Yorkshire section of the Leeds &
Liverpool Canal follows the River Aire valley
for 30 miles between Skipton and Leeds. It has distinctive
architectural features such as several staircase locks, the most
famous being the Five Rise Locks at Bingley. There are also around 40
swing bridges on this section, which (along with 29 locks) does not make
for rapid cruising. Boaters should also be aware that there are time
restrictions for using locks in the Leeds area because of safety and water
conservation, and the 13 locks between Newlay and River Lock in Leeds
can only be used in daylight hours. Many of the locks and swing bridges
will require a handcuff key to open them. Your hard work will be rewarded
by superb scenery all the way to the outskirts of Leeds. Attractions such
as Saltaire village, Kirkstall Abbey, East Riddlesden Hall and the Armley
Mills Industrial Museum make the journey a rewarding one.

Skipton to Bingley

Skipton announces itself as 'The Gateway to the Yorkshire Dales', which has been made apparent by the beautiful open countryside surrounding the canal since leaving Gargrave. An ancient market town, Skipton once traded in sheep but now has a market open to the public four days a week. It has many attractions, including Skipton Castle (one of the best-preserved medieval castles in England) and the town has become a major draw for tourists.

From Skipton Wharf you can follow the Springs Branch that passes through a narrow gorge to Skipton Castle, which towers high above the water. The canal was built to carry limestone from Lord Thanet's quarries but has not been used for this purpose since they closed in 1946. Only boats shorter than 35 feet can cruise this branch because of restricted turning space at the end. The best way to explore it is on foot,

Springs Branch at Skipton.

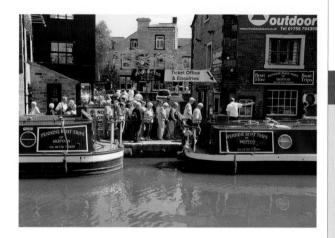

Trip boats leave from the Pennine Cruiser base at Skipton Canal Basin.

Fred Trueman

A recent addition to the canal scene in Skipton is a statue of former Yorkshire and England cricketer Fred Trueman. Universally known as 'Fiery Fred', he was one of the greatest fast bowlers in cricketing history and the first to take 300 wickets in a Test career. The bronze statue of him in action was erected by the canal basin in 2010. Fred, who was a local resident in his later years, died in 2006.

following the towpath to the castle and then going on into Skipton Wood. Another highlight of the branch is the acclaimed Stanforth's – Celebrated Pork Pie Establishment, which is next to the canal.

The annual Skipton Waterway Festival is based at Skipton Canal Basin, where trip boats operate and you can find the excellent Bizzie Lizzie's fish and chippy by the bridge.

The next part of our journey is the section between Skipton and Bingley, which was the first part of the canal to open, in 1773. Soon after leaving Skipton, it is time to negotiate the first of many swing bridges. At Snaygill there is a boatyard where narrowboats can be hired, followed by a lovely section of woodland aglow with masses of bluebells in the springtime. This opens out to a steep hillside at Farnhill, where a tower at the top of the hill gives wide views across the Aire Valley towards distant moorland.

The canal continues to Kildwick, which has a small aqueduct above a street in the village. Beyond that there is a two-mile section with five swing bridges before you reach Silsden, a mill town that retains some old mills and warehouses to remind us of its industrial past. Silsden's numerous shops make it a good place for boaters to stock up, and its boatyard offers narrowboat hire. Walkers can wet their whistles at the local pubs, and there is a number of good

The Fred Trueman statue at Skipton Wharf.

TOP **Moorland scenery at Farnhill.**

ABOVE **View from the town bridge at Silsden.**

restaurants. It also once had the honour (according to Guinness World Records) of being the place where Britain's biggest onion, weighing in at an impressive 14lb, was grown.

The canal continues southwards along the Aire Valley, with hills to the north and the rooftops of Keighley to the west. There are no locks in the 17 miles between Gargrave and Bingley, but swing bridges appear with monotonous regularity. Some of these electrically operated bridges are over roads so boaters should make sure they understand procedure to avoid holding up traffic.

It's worth stopping at Riddlesden to see East Riddlesden Hall, a 17th-century manor house with beautiful gardens, owned by the National Trust. This is also a good place from which to visit Keighley, which is about a mile away, and take a ride on the Keighley and Worth Valley Railway, which became famous as the location for the film *The Railway*

Children. From Keighley station you can take a steam train to Haworth, home of the Brontë family.

As the canal approaches Bingley, the environs become progressively built-up and the moorland views towards Ilkley in the north disappear. From the top, the first view of the vertiginous drop at Bingley Five Rise Locks can set the senses reeling for boaters and walkers alike. Boaters can relax as the complex procedure of operating the staircase locks will be done by a resident lock-keeper. In the five locks, one chamber leads directly into the next one, hence the term 'staircase'. The locks raise or drop the canal 60 feet and provide much spectator interest for the many walkers who use the towpath. A cafe and shop are housed in an old stable block at the top of the locks and, once at the bottom, boaters will find more staircase locks just around the next bend. This time the locks are arranged in a three-rise staircase. Apart from its locks, Bingley is famous for the manufacture of thermal underwear in a factory that overlooks the canal.

BELOW **Checking the operation of a swing bridge before opening it.**

BOTTOM **Bingley Five Rise Locks.**

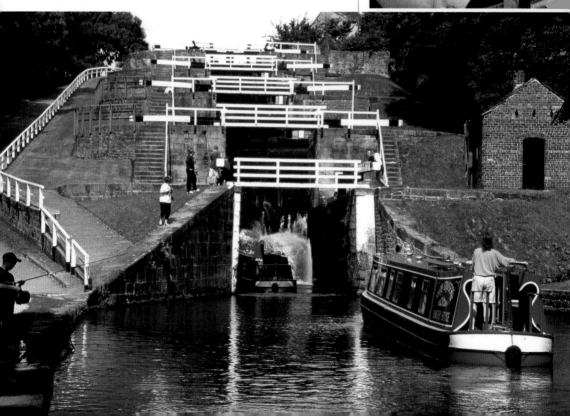

Bingley to Leeds

After Bingley comes Dowley Gap, which has a seven-arched aqueduct over the River Aire, a pair of staircase locks and a pub with fine views over the Aire Valley from its patio. A lovely wooded section follows, leading to a single lock, and the canal then arrives at Saltaire.

Saltaire was founded in 1853 by Victorian entrepreneur Sir Titus Salt when he moved the production of wool from his Bradford factory to a site that was at that time undeveloped countryside. He built his mills and a model village for his workers based on a similar plan to that of the Cadbury village at Bournville, and the canal provided transportation for his goods to the Port of Liverpool. His workers, released from the Bradford slums, had everything they needed, with one exception – a pub! Salt was a deeply religious man who believed in temperance. The village is a UNESCO World Heritage site and the Salts Mill is now home to one of the largest collections of work by local artist David Hockney. The mill also has a shopping area with a large bookshop plus several restaurants and cafes. Before leaving Saltaire, take a ride on the funicular Shipley Glen Tramway, which has open carriages taking you 2,000 feet down through woodland to a park with river walks.

The next stop is Shipley, where you can see the junction of the former Bradford Canal. In 1866, the Bradford Canal was described as 'a seething cauldron of impurity', mostly because of raw sewage pollution, and was condemned as a health hazard. It reopened again ten years later, but was finally abandoned in 1922. Parts of the original line can still be seen and there are plans to rebuild the canal for leisure purposes.

Shipley's waterside houses a mixture of old warehouses and new buildings. Apollo Canal Cruises, who operate a waterbus service between Shipley and Bingley, are based in a converted warehouse.

The New Mill at Saltaire.

Leaving Shipley, the canal takes a wide bend to the north with the three Field Locks at the apex of the curve. The locks are set beside hilly woodland, making it difficult to remember you are really not very far from Bradford's urban sprawl. The nearby village of Esholt (once used as the setting for television's Emmerdale soap opera) can be reached by a path from Bridge 211. More swing bridges follow before you reach the two Dobson Locks at Apperley Bridge. There are facilities for boaters by the Canal & River Trust's maintenance yard, and more a little further on at a marina.

Afterwards the canal curves around the edge of the beautiful Calverley Wood, where stone was once quarried and carried away on barges. Next comes Rodley Bridge with two canalside pubs and more swing bridges. The canal and the River Aire are now close companions, curving around

ABOVE **Swing bridge at Apperley Bridge.**

BELOW **Converted warehouses at Shipley.**

TOP **Newlay Locks.**

ABOVE **Office Lock at Leeds.**

woodland to three staircase locks and a marina at Newlay. Like Calverley, the woodland around Newlay Locks conceals former stone quarries that used the canal for transportation. Newlay Locks are soon followed by three more at Forge Three Rise, by which time the outskirts of Leeds are closing in around the waterway.

This wooded section of canal is a very pleasant way to enter the city of Leeds. Through the trees you will see the attractive ruins of Kirkstall Abbey on the opposite side of the river. The Abbey has a museum situated in its gatehouse featuring its history, and a reconstructed Victorian street with shops and cottages. Just beyond Kirkstall Lock is the impressive Kirkstall Brewery, which has now been converted to student accommodation.

Next comes the Leeds Industrial Museum at Armley Mills, which encapsulates the city's industrial history under the roof of what was once the world's largest woollen mill. Its many working exhibits include textile machinery, water wheels and steam engines. In 1801 there were only 20 factories in Leeds, but by 1838 there were more than 100 woollen mills employing 10,000 people. This huge expansion transformed Leeds into a major industrial city and the canal played its part in transportation.

The second half of the 19th century saw Leeds become the leading manufacturers of ready-made clothing for companies such as Marks and Spencer, Burtons and Hepworths, who became household names. Printing and packaging was another important local industry in the late 19th century, with 8,000 people employed in the trade by the turn of the century.

After Armley Mills, the canal continues to Spring Garden Lock and Oddy Lock, passing a variety of old and new buildings. At Office Lock the canal is overlooked on one side by a factory built in Italianate style with campanile towers, and a railway viaduct on the other.

Leeds Central railway station is just around the corner from Granary Wharf, which was extensively redeveloped in 2009. Granary Wharf is now home to hotels, pubs and canalside apartment blocks, with shops and restaurants in an area known as 'The Dark Arches' beneath the railway viaduct. Leeds' revitalised waterfront now attracts thousands of visitors, in complete contrast to the run-down strip of disused factories and grimy water that once made this area a place to avoid. Away from the waterside, the city has many attractions that include Leeds Town Hall, Leeds Corn Exchange, markets, theatres and the Victorian shopping arcades.

The Leeds & Liverpool Canal ends its long journey at River Lock and gives way to the Aire & Calder Navigation.

practical information

Distance: Skipton to Leeds is 30 miles with 29 locks.

Boaters: Many of the locks are arranged in staircases, which means one lock leads directly into its neighbour. There are no tunnels but there are some 40 swing bridges that are either manually or electrically operated.

Walkers: The canal has a continuous towpath so there are no problems for walkers. The canal follows the River Aire Valley and so does the railway between Skipton and Leeds. There are several stations on the route situated at varying distances from the canal; check on a map.

Places of interest: Skipton Castle; East Riddlesden Hall; Saltaire; and Kirkstall Abbey.

Key pubs: There are numerous good waterside pubs throughout this section of the Leeds & Liverpool Canal.

One of the Victorian shopping arcades in Leeds.

'Tom Puddings' at Pollington in March 1969.

Chapter 12

AIRE & CALDER NAVIGATION

AND SHEFFIELD & SOUTH YORKSHIRE NAVIGATION

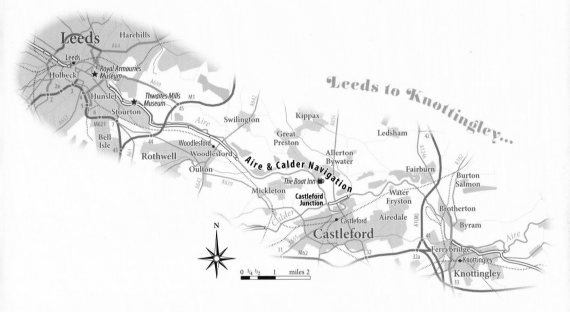

The River Aire was first made navigable from Knottingley to Leeds in 1700, and was an immediate commercial success, transporting coal from Yorkshire's coalfields and bringing in raw materials for the expanding woollen industry. By 1750 trade had increased to such an extent that the poorly maintained river navigation could no longer cope with all the traffic. New sections of canal were cut and new locks were added. These improvements, along with the arrival of the Leeds & Liverpool Canal in 1816, brought a further increase in commercial activity. The size of the canal soon became inadequate as cargoes got larger and a new, wider canal between Knottingley and Goole opened in 1826.

Map continues on page 147.

If the textile industry was the spur for building this canal, it was coal that made it prosperous and coal was the main commodity on the waterway until recent times. In 1862 William Bartholomew, chief engineer of the Aire & Calder Navigation Company, designed a compartment boat for carrying bulk coal. He introduced the new designs in 1864 and they soon became known as 'Tom Puddings'. The derivation of the name is a bit of a mystery but the 'Tom' part could originate from William Bartholomew's father, a former canal-company engineer who was called Tom. The 'Pudding' bit is anyone's guess – maybe deriving from the users' love of Yorkshire Puddings!

Each boat carried around 35 tons and up to 20 of them were coupled into trains and pulled by a tug. During the First World War nearly 2,000,000 tons of coal were carried on the canal in 1,000 compartment boats. This total was maintained right into the 1950s when British Waterways reported in their house magazine *Waterways* that 2,000,000 tons were carried on the canal in 1955. 'Tom Puddings' remained a feature of the Aire & Calder Navigation until 1986, when they were discontinued after trade in the Yorkshire coalfield declined because of the miners' strike.

In later years, oil, sand and gravel became important commodities carried on the waterway. All the Aire & Calder Navigation locks are mechanised and many are operated by lock-keepers from waterside control rooms. Lock-keepers, who are employed to assist commercial traffic, often help pleasure craft through the locks too. Otherwise, all locks can be self-operated but boaters should obey traffic lights and remember this is still a commercial waterway.

Leeds to Castleford

This navigation begins at the tail of River Lock. The first section of the Aire & Calder Navigation was dominated by the huge Tetley Brewery, which closed in 2008 after the business moved to Northampton. This section of waterfront, once lined with warehouses and wharves, has been replaced by modern housing. Next comes the handsome Crown Point Bridge, which crosses the River Aire in front of Leeds Lock and the entrance to Clarence Dock. This is the location of the Royal Armouries Museum and its huge collection of arms and weaponry, some of which was previously held in the Tower of London. The museum stands beside the rebuilt Clarence Dock, and visiting boats can find moorings and other boating facilities, as well as a supermarket and restaurants.

Leeds Lock is overlooked by a collection of modern buildings, with the Royal Armouries Museum on one side and apartment blocks on the other. After Leeds Lock, the

The Royal Armouries Museum at Clarence Dock.

navigation progresses to Knostrop, passing a number of old warehouses. At Knostrop Flood Lock boaters must take the central channel, avoiding a weir and an arm that once led to an oil terminal. The lock should remain open at all times, except after heavy rain when the navigation is liable to flood.

A freight depot run by British Waterways, once busy but now disused, is followed by a mechanised lock and then, at Stourton, the Thwaite Mills Watermill Museum, run by Leeds City Council. This former flint and chinastone grinding mill opened to the public as a museum in 1990, and visitors can see an impressive working waterwheel.

This section of waterway, once dominated by a huge power station, is now home to industrial estates and a container depot. The Leeds suburbs are left behind and beyond the motorway viaduct a hint of countryside appears. The navigation proceeds to Fishpond Lock and then on to Woodlesford, passing an area that was formerly used for opencast mining. The attractive Woodlesford Lock has bird

Leeds Waterfront Heritage Trail near Knostrop Flood Lock.

hides nearby and is close to the village, where you will find pubs, shops and a post office.

In 1988, following a breach in the river near Woodlesford, a new section was built. This diverted the line of the navigation to include a new lock at Lemonroyd, which replaced the old Lemonroyd Lock and Kippax Lock. New bridges and a basin that now supports a marina were also built. Oil tankers can still be seen unloading at an oil terminal by the bridge above Lemonroyd Lock and Lemonroyd Marina. Stop here to visit the Water Haigh Woodland Park, a large nature reserve with lakes created on the site of a former colliery. This links up with St Aidan's washland nature reserve and Rothwell Country Park, providing a green corridor into the city of Leeds, all on reclaimed industrial land.

The next three miles of waterway pass through open countryside, with lakes on either side. At Allerton Bywater, The Boat inn had a ferry that carried miners across the navigation from their homes in Methley and Mickletown to work in the pit at Allerton at a charge of sixpence a week.

An old poem states that 'Castleford women must needs be

Henry Moore

Castleford's biggest claim to fame is that it is the birthplace of the sculptor Henry Moore, famous throughout the world for his large abstract bronze sculptures often displayed in public places.

The Castleford Forum, a new development in the town's Carnegie Library, tells the story of Moore's early life and has one of his sculptures on display. The Forum also tells the story of Castleford's development from Roman times, when it was called Legioleum. The Henry Moore Institute in Leeds displays some of his work, alongside other exhibitions of sculpture.

fair, Because they wash both in Calder and Aire'. Indeed the Rivers Calder and Aire do meet at Castleford Junction but there is no guarantee you will find lines of glamorous local girls waiting to meet you at the lock side. The first concern for boaters at the junction is to turn left into the lock and not go straight ahead, where there is a dangerous weir. Opposite the junction is the entrance to the Calder section of the Aire & Calder Navigation, which leads to Wakefield and then on to Huddersfield and Sowerby Bridge. Both the Huddersfield Canal and Rochdale Canal eventually reach Manchester and provide an alternative route to the Leeds & Liverpool Canal.

Castleford was once an important industrial town surrounded by coalmines, all of which closed after the miners' strike in 1984. A large chemical works, potteries, a chocolate factory and even Allinson's flour mill have all now closed, though Allinson's will reopen at some stage as a working mill and heritage centre. Castleford might not be home to any mines today, but it does have a huge leisure complex called Xscape, which boasts Europe's largest indoor real-snow ski-slope. Xscape Castleford also has 14 cinemas, a bowling alley, mini-golf and a lot of restaurants. From the lock, Castleford's many delights can be reached by the long footbridge that crosses the river next to Allinson's Mill.

Woodlesford Lock.

Castleford to Knottingley

Castleford Flood Lock should remain open except during periods of heavy rain. However, there are traffic control lights that must be observed at all times as this is a still a commercial waterway and colliding head-on with a loaded sand barge could have dire consequences. There is usually a motley collection of boats and barges moored along the banks between Castleford Lock and Bulholme Lock. After Bulholme Lock, the navigation winds past the site of several abandoned collieries that are currently being landscaped. There is no recognised towpath on this section for four miles between Bulholme Lock and Ferrybridge, but there is a series of footpaths that can be followed on the north side of the navigation via RSPB Fairburn Ings nature reserve, which is well worth visiting. Boaters should note that there are no mooring facilities at RSPB Fairburn Ings.

Ferrybridge Lock, looking towards the power station.

Kings Mill flour mill at Knottingley.

It's hard to imagine that the old bridge at Ferrybridge, built in 1803, once carried the A1 trunk road. It was replaced by a dual carriageway viaduct, which in turn has been updated by a motorway bridge that crosses the Aire above the power station. The old bridge now supports a footpath and gives you a good view of Ferrybridge 'C' Power Station with its giant cooling towers. Until the last load of coal was delivered in December 2002, you could have stood here to watch coal barges being unloaded into the power station, but the outlook is now green and landscaped. Ferrybridge has a good waterside pub at the end of the lock cut.

After Ferrybridge Lock you leave the River Aire Navigation and enter a canalised section between Ferrybridge and Goole. At Knottingley, there is an imposing flour mill, and Harker's boatbuilding yard. The waterside is lined with factories and housing, but at Cow Lane Bridge residents have brightened up the canal environs by planting flowers along the towpath.

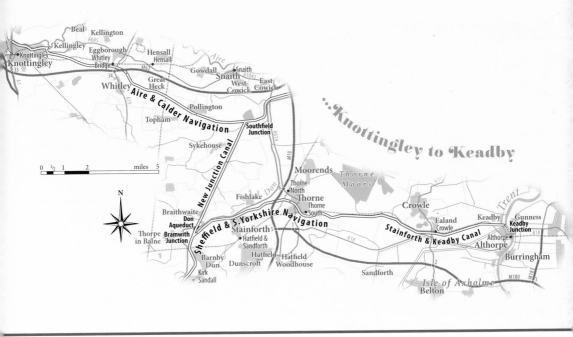

Knottingley to Bramwith

The canal turns right at Bank Dole Junction. Ahead is Bank
Dole Lock, which leads into the Aire Navigation and then to
the Selby Canal, eventually going to York via the River
Ouse. The Aire & Calder Navigation soon leaves Knottingley
behind and at Stubbs Bridge you pass near Kellingley
Colliery, the last working coal mine in this area, but now
subject to closure in 2015.

Now the canal heads out into the countryside to Whitley
Bridge. For the next eight miles the canal passes through a
flat landscape devoid of woodland, emphasising the bleakness
of the surroundings. For most of the journey the canal is
accompanied by the M62 motorway and at Whitley Lock the
cooling towers of Eggborough Power Station are prominent

ABOVE **An empty barge returning to Goole Docks.**

RIGHT **At Pollington, the lock-keeper controls the gates from his elevated cabin.**

above the fields. Unfortunately, the commercial traffic, once so prolific on this section, has severely diminished. At one time, trains of coal-carrying 'Tom Puddings', oil tankers, and sand and gravel barges would sometimes queue to pass through the locks at Whitley and Pollington; now most of the boating activity along this length comes from pleasure craft based at the South Yorkshire Boat Club at Goole.

At Southfield Junction you turn right on to the New Junction Canal. The Aire & Calder Navigation main line goes on for another six miles to Goole, where there are extensive docks and a waterways museum.

The New Junction Canal was built in 1905 and connects the Aire & Calder Navigation to the South Yorkshire Navigation. It is five-and-a-half miles long and dead straight for its entire length. It has one lock, two aqueducts and five lift or swing bridges. The aqueducts are at each end – one crossing the River Went at the north end and another crossing the River Don at the south end. The Don Aqueduct has two guillotine gates to prevent the river from overflowing into the canal and flooding miles of surrounding countryside.

Sykehouse Lock has a manually operated swing bridge across the lock chamber, which must be opened before the electrically powered gates will work. The canal then passes through a sparsely populated area with just two small villages and no waterside pubs. There are no boating facilities until Bramwith on the Stainforth & Keadby Canal. Kirk Bramwith village has an interesting church that dates back to medieval times and is worth a visit. The New Junction joins the Stainforth & Keadby Canal on a very sharp left turn soon after crossing the Don Aqueduct. The cooling towers of Thorpe Marsh Power Station dominated this flat countryside for miles until they were demolished in 2012.

The Don Aqueduct.

Bramwith to Keadby

The Stainforth & Keadby Canal forms the eastern section of the Sheffield & South Yorkshire Navigation. The distance between Bramwith and Keadby is 15 miles, with three locks. The first lock at Bramwith comes soon after the very tight turn out of the New Junction Canal. Bramwith Lock has two working chambers so boaters should check which one is in use that day. There are basic facilities such as a water point and toilet at the lock.

The canal and the River Don become close companions until they reach Stainforth and its waterside pub. Afterwards, river and canal part company as the Don goes north to Goole and the canal passes beneath the M18 motorway to Thorne.

Stainforth & Keadby Canal at Bramwith.

ABOVE **The River Don at Stainforth.**

LEFT **The waterfront at Thorne.**

BELOW **Wykewell Lift Bridge.**

Thorne has a busy waterfront with two marinas and a boatyard. There is a pub and restaurant by the bridge, which gives access to the town-centre shops. Thorne is the birthplace of the operatic soprano Lesley Garrett.

The electrically operated Wykewell Lift Bridge carries a road, so barriers have to be dropped to stop traffic.

Once Thorne has been left behind, the canal passes through a flat landscape full of dykes and drains, which stretches for miles in either direction. Just beyond Moores Swing Bridge you can see a number of farms still using a medieval method of strip farming, whereby each owner's narrow strip of land is separated from its neighbour by a

OPPOSITE **Keadby Lock.**

BELOW **Dead-straight canal at Crowle Wharf.**

practical information

⊟ **Distance:** Leeds to Keadby is 47 miles with 16 locks.

Boaters: You need to remember that the Aire & Calder Navigation is still recognised as a commercial waterway, although these days barges are few and far between.

Walkers: There is no recognised towpath between Bulholme Lock at Castleford and Ferrybridge, but the towpath is otherwise continuous. There is a railway service between Leeds and Castleford. Knottingley and Whitley Bridge are connected by rail and the railway follows the Stainforth & Keadby Canal for its entire length, with intermittent stations.

Places of interest: The Royal Armouries Museum at Leeds and Thwaites Mills Museum at Stourton.

Key pubs: The Boat Inn at Allerton Bywater.

small dyke. The canal is then accompanied by the railway all the way to Keadby, about eight miles away. The windmills of a wind farm follow the canal for some distance, taking advantage of the exposed flat landscape. This north-western corner of North Lincolnshire has the collective name of the Isle of Axholme, and the only notable habitation near the canal in this empty region is the village of Crowle. Crowle is a one-mile walk along the road from Crowle Wharf, but there are no other villages or waterside pubs until Keadby.

Just before Keadby, the railway crosses the canal by the Vazon Sliding Railway Bridge, only a few feet above the water. It is controlled from a nearby signal box and boaters must wait until there is a long enough gap between trains before the bridge can be opened. The bridge then slides sideways to allow boats to pass. You will see Keadby Power Station and Keadby Lock, which is operated by a lock-keeper and leads into the River Trent. It is advisable to give the lock-keeper 24 hours' notice before arrival.

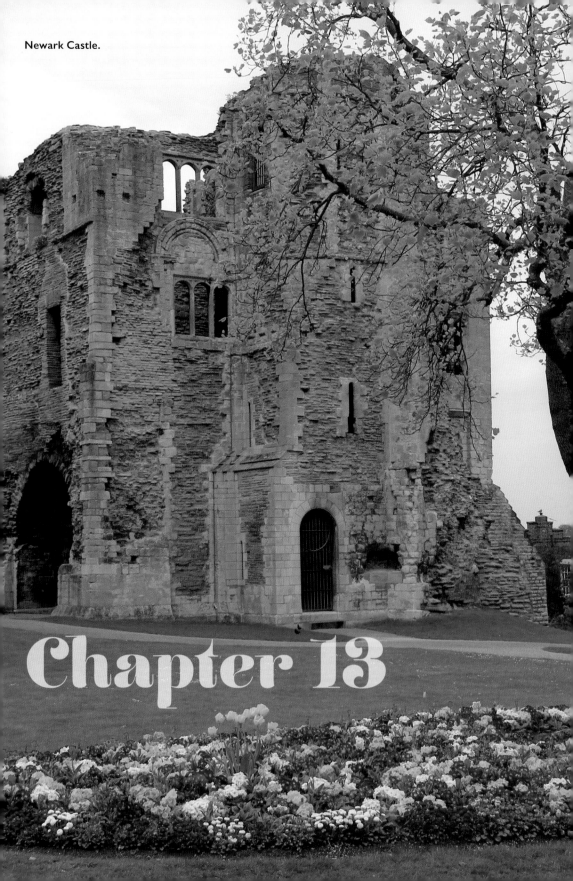

Newark Castle.

Chapter 13

RIVER TRENT

"Keadby to Cromwell Lock..."

The River Trent is navigable for 94 miles from its confluence with the Humber to Derwent Mouth, where it meets the Trent & Mersey Canal. It divides into two sections, with Cromwell Lock at the point where the navigable tidal river gives way to the non-tidal higher reaches. On this journey you join the Trent at Keadby, where boats still have about 40 miles of tidal river before reaching Cromwell Lock. There is a number of safe havens where boats can moor up on the journey, but any boater wishing to reach Cromwell Lock in one go must take advice from the lock-keeper at Keadby. The tidal section must be treated with great respect, especially after heavy rain. Although the traffic has considerably reduced, the tidal Trent is still a commercial river and an encounter with a loaded sand barge can concentrate the mind of even the most experienced canal boater. The tidal river mainly passes through flat countryside so the banks are usually quite high, but above Cromwell Lock the surroundings become more attractive, with pretty wooded sections and interesting villages.

Map continues on page 161.

Keadby to Gainsborough

After leaving Keadby Lock turn right on to the tidal Trent. Boaters should inform the Keadby lock-keeper if their intention is to reach Cromwell Lock in one day as he will inform the lock-keeper at Cromwell to alert him if they do not arrive. Should boaters change their plan and decide to break their passage by mooring up for the night at a recognised sheltered place, they must inform the Cromwell lock-keeper.

At Keadby there is a road and rail bridge, followed by the M18 motorway viaduct. Otherwise there is not a lot to see before the twin villages of East and West Butterwick, which face each other across the river. The high flood banks make it difficult to see much of the flat Isle of Axholme, which stretches away for miles on either side. Apart from the

Entering the River Trent from Keadby Lock.

motorway, there are no road crossings for 17 miles between Keadby and Gainsborough.

Occasionally there will be a glimpse of a small hamlet on the riverbank, but there is no safe access for boats until reaching West Stockwith Basin, which marks the start of the Chesterfield Canal.

The lock at West Stockwith is manned and the keeper's advice may be required if the tidal flow makes access to the basin difficult. West Stockwith Basin has moorings and a pub with a restaurant. Nearby, huge steel gates mark the entrance to the River Idle. In theory the river is navigable as far as Bawtry and was once an important trading link between the Trent and some South Yorkshire towns. The Idle has since been diverted by drainage engineers, so now it lives up to its name and is no longer used for commercial traffic. The Chesterfield Canal is navigable for 32 miles, with a further 12 miles under restoration that will eventually reconnect the town of Chesterfield with the River Trent.

TOP **West Stockwith Lock.**

ABOVE **The M18 motorway crossing.**

Beyond West Stockwith there is little change in the riverside scenery until Gainsborough, the largest town on the tidal Trent. The town achieved the status of a port in 1841, and at that time it was the most inland port in England, being nearly 60 miles from the sea. Gainsborough became an important industrial town, with Marshall's engineering company exporting tractors and steam engines all over Europe. Another company, founded by William Rose, invented the first packaging machine and this achievement is commemorated by a plaque in the town centre. Marshall's closed in the 1980s and the 16-acre site is now occupied by a shopping area known as Marshall's Yard. The town's single river bridge is called Gainsborough's Arches, and many of the industrial buildings on the riverbank have been demolished or converted to new uses. A riverside walk has been created and a water festival takes place annually.

Riverside walk at Gainsborough.

Gainsborough to Cromwell Lock

Continuing south from Gainsborough, the river starts to bend as the flat landscape is left behind. Low hills and woodland on the banks appear as the river reaches Torksey. There are safe moorings on the approach to Torksey Lock, which leads into the Fossdyke Navigation. The 43-mile-long navigation links Lincoln and Boston to the Trent. Torksey Lock has a pub and a visitor centre. In the nearby village, there is a ruined 16th-century manor house known as Torksey Castle.

The cooling towers of Cottam Power Station dominate the landscape opposite Torksey Lock, and one of the features in the next few miles are various other power stations

Waterside garden at Torksey Lock.

overlooking the riverside. After Torksey Lock comes Dunham Toll Bridge, which is the first road crossing over the river since Gainsborough 15 miles away. There are safe moorings here, in fact the last ones until Cromwell Lock. Leaving Dunham, the river has more twists and turns but the landscape remains generally flat with several sand and gravel pits and another large power station.

At this point the safe haven of Cromwell Lock finally looms into view, heralding the start of the non-tidal section of the river. The setting of the lock is remote, with moorings and a large weir thundering next to it. It was here that ten soldiers of the Royal Engineers drowned while on a training exercise in 1975, and there is a memorial garden with a block of granite bearing their names at the side of the lock. The lock is enormous, has a resident lock-keeper, and is big enough to hold several barges.

Cromwell Lock.

Cromwell Lock
to Nottingham

After Cromwell Lock travelling is easier for boaters as the non-tidal river becomes more friendly and the scenery becomes increasingly varied and attractive. Now you can stop at villages such as North Muskham, with its riverside pub, 12th-century church and a nature reserve that is popular with birdwatchers.

Once past the bridge carrying the A1 trunk road you enter Newark in a maze of road and railway bridges criss-crossing a navigation that has seen very few bridges since

ABOVE **Newark Castle.**

BELOW **Newark Town Lock.**

leaving Keadby. Now follows a lock, a marina, old maltings and a new footbridge before reaching Newark Castle and Town Lock. The first castle at Newark was built in 1130, and it has seen many changes over the centuries. King John died here in 1216 and it was a Royalist stronghold during the Civil War. Now in ruins, it remains an impressive edifice viewed from Town Lock or the stone bridge that leads into the town centre. The town has a Georgian marketplace surrounded by old buildings, and a group of old warehouses above Town Lock still proudly bear their original names, such as Trent Navigation Co and Newark Egg Packers.

Before leaving Newark you pass another marina and after a series of convoluted bends you arrive at Farndon. Looking back to Newark from the bends you get a good view of the town's rooftops, which are dominated by the 250-feet-high spire of the Church of St Mary Magdalene. Farndon is a pretty village with a marina, two good pubs and a restaurant.

The navigation continues on its serpentine course to Fiskerton, the home of various Iron Age finds over the years, as well as a pub and a shop. Next comes Hazelford Lock, followed by the most attractive section of the entire navigation with the wooded Trent Hills to the east and a series of lakes on flat land to the west. In the springtime, wild flowers adorn both banks with colourful displays. Later in the year the forested cliffs of the Trent Hills make a superb backdrop to the riverside with their autumn colours.

This lovely stretch of river is followed by Gunthorpe. Boasting a busy waterfront with pubs, restaurants, a marina and a boatyard, it isn't surprising that the village has become a popular weekend retreat for people in Nottingham who want a few hours away from the city. Boaters should be wary of the wide weir before entering the lock. Gunthorpe Bridge is the only crossing point over the river between Newark and Nottingham.

ABOVE **Trent Hills near Gunthorpe.**

BELOW **Gunthorpe Bridge.**

ABOVE **White-water canoeing course at Holme Pierrepont.**

BELOW **Trent Bridge in Nottingham.**

Beyond Gunthorpe, the navigation continues its winding course to Stoke Bardolph and the Ferry Boat Inn, named after a former ferry crossing. You then continue on to Stoke Lock, delightfully situated beneath steep wooded cliffs that conceal the town of Radcliffe on Trent from the river. The outskirts of Nottingham now appear as the navigation reaches Holme Lock. Colwick Marina and Colwick Country Park are on one side, while the National Water Sports Centre at Holme Pierrepont is on the other. A six-lane rowing course, a white-water canoe slalom course and sailing are among the many attractions at Holme Pierrepont.

The navigation continues towards Trent Bridge, leaving the river at Meadow Lane Lock (which is the start of the Nottingham Canal). Trent Bridge can be seen just beyond the lock and Nottingham Forest FC's football stadium is on the

Fellows, Morton & Clayton Ltd

The company was founded in 1837 by James Fellows, who was then based at West Bromwich and Tipton in the Black Country. By 1860 the company had expanded to 50 boats, and Frederick Morton became a partner in 1876. By the time Thomas Clayton joined the company in 1889, Fellows, Morton and Clayton (FMC), as it was then called, had a fleet of over 120 boats. The company headquarters was in Birmingham and, at the peak of its carrying heyday, it had 31 depots of varying sizes scattered throughout the waterway system. Joshua Fellows, son of the founder, introduced a fleet of steam-driven narrowboats that became known as 'joshers', and one remaining FMC steamboat *President* can still be seen at waterway rallies representing the Black Country Living Museum.

In 1895, new offices, stables and warehouses opened in Nottingham and these can be seen today, albeit being used for other purposes as the company ceased trading in 1947. One of the buildings became a waterways museum, but this was not successful and closed in 1998. Another building is a pub and restaurant that acquired the FMC name and has moorings and waterside seating.

ABOVE Fellows, Morton & Clayton pub sign.

LEFT Fellows, Morton & Clayton pub in Nottingham.

opposite side of the river from Meadow Lane Lock. Trent Bridge cricket ground is on the far side of the bridge facing a riverside landscaped area with trees and gardens.

The 15-mile-long Nottingham Canal opened in 1796, connecting the Cromford Canal at Langley Mill to Nottingham and the Trent. Most of the line closed in 1937, with the exception of the Nottingham section, which has remained open and is an integral part of the Trent Navigation's passage through the city. Once through Meadow Lane Lock, the canal heads towards the city centre taking a sharp left turn at Poplar Arm. This section is overlooked by housing and hotels and leads to Carrington Street Bridge, next to the central station. Here you will see the fine old

OPPOSITE **Former British Waterways warehouse in Nottingham.**

BELOW **Fellows, Morton & Clayton Ltd livery.**

Registered at Birmingham No 1475

FELLOWS, MORTON 1396 & CLAYTON LTD.

warehouses that were once the Nottingham depot of Fellows, Morton & Clayton Ltd, the largest and most famous of all the canal carrying fleets.

A few years ago, the canal in the centre of the city had become a depressing, gloomy, run-down area. It has since been revitalised without losing too many of its original buildings, and is now one of Nottingham's visitor attractions. Castle Lock is not only overlooked by Nottingham Castle, but also by a towering six-storey warehouse that once belonged to British Waterways and retains the lettering to prove it.

Nottingham Castle Marina has all facilities for visiting boaters and there is a pub, a supermarket, restaurants and a retail park all within easy reach. The city centre – with all its shopping possibilities – is close by and so is Nottingham

Sawley Locks.

Castle, which dates back to 1069. Visit the Nottingham Castle Museum and Art Gallery then stop for a drink at Ye Olde Trip To Jerusalem pub beneath the castle walls, reputed to be the oldest inn in England. There is also the Lace Centre and the City of Caves in the Broadmarsh Centre. The legend of Robin Hood is never far away and a statue of him stands near the castle. All these places are just a short walk from the canal.

Lenton Chain is where the Nottingham Canal used to turn right and go north, and its name comes from the fact that the canal company used to lock the entrance to the canal at weekends to stop unauthorised users from gaining access. This is where the Nottingham Canal gives way to the Beeston Cut that gradually moves away from central Nottingham. The first section of the cut is totally dominated by the huge Boots industrial estate, but after passing through Beeston Lock you return to the River Trent (where there is a marina) and the river runs alongside the Attenborough Nature Reserve. This provides a welcome return to open countryside, with a series of large lakes made up from disused gravel pits. The reserve was opened in 1966 by Sir David Attenborough, but the name actually comes from the village of Attenborough that is adjacent to the reserve. It is a haven for waterfowl and migrant birds.

The next section of river, popular with boats from local sailing clubs, leads to Cranfleet Lock. From here the short Cranfleet Cut leads out into the wide-open space of Trent Lock Junction. Overlooked by the cooling towers of Ratcliffe-on-Soar Power Station the River Trent is joined from the south by the River Soar Navigation, while to the north lies the entrance to the Erewash Canal. Go straight ahead to the paired Sawley Locks and on to Sawley Marina, which has all boating facilities. After passing under the M1 motorway viaduct, you reach Derwent Mouth Lock, which marks the boundary between the navigation and the start of the Trent & Mersey Canal. The actual terminus of the Trent Navigation is at Cavendish Bridge, next to Shardlow Marina.

practical information

Distance: Keadby to Shardlow is 85 miles with 11 locks.

Boaters: The section of river between Keadby and Gainsborough Arches is administered by Associated British Ports. Beyond that it is the responsibility of the Canal & River Trust. A VHF band radio is an important aid when navigating the tidal waterway, and extra care must be taken throughout this section, as it is still a commercial waterway. An aegir or tidal bore may be encountered between Keadby and Gainsborough. This can vary in height up to 5 feet and is often seen with spring tides.

Walkers: There is a continuous footpath from Trent Lock through Nottingham to Meadow Lane Lock. Then there is a towpath all the way to the A1 bridge north of Newark, but in places the path changes sides and there is no longer a ferry. Beyond Newark there is nothing until Cromwell Lock, where there is a path but once again it changes sides with no available ferry, so it can't be used as a continuous footpath.

Places of interest: Newark Castle; Nottingham Castle; and Holme Pierrepont water sports centre.

Key pubs: Ferry Boat Inn at Stoke Bardolph; The Riverside Pub at Farndon; and The Muskham Ferry at Newark.

Chapter 14

The Trent & Mersey
Canal at Willington.

TRENT & MERSEY CANAL

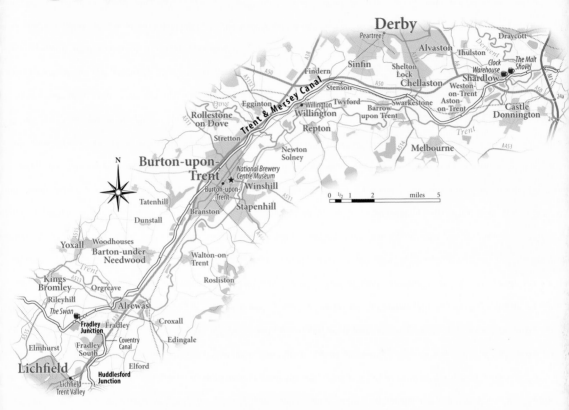

After the wide River Trent and the broad locks on the northern canals
we return to the world of the narrow canal that we left at the opposite
end of the Trent & Mersey Canal between Middlewich and Preston Brook
Tunnel. The next three waterways, the Trent & Mersey Canal, Coventry
Canal and the Oxford Canal, are all examples of Brindley's early canals
and were built in the second half of the 18th century. The locks between
Shardlow and Stenson are wide beam, but after that there are narrow
locks all the way. Apart from the passage through Burton upon Trent,
most of the journey is through pleasant countryside that is often wooded
and stands in complete contrast to the flat surroundings and high flood
banks on the tidal section of the River Trent.

Shardlow to Burton upon Trent

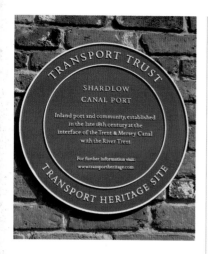

BELOW **The Clock Warehouse at Shardlow, now a pub and restaurant.**

Shardlow became an inland port when the Trent & Mersey Canal was connected to the River Trent. Before that there was nothing at Shardlow apart from a few scattered farms. Once the canal arrived, riverboats had to tranship their cargoes to canal boats, so warehouses were built. Slowly a town developed around the port, with houses for the workers. Shops and inns soon followed and so Shardlow became a busy new town.

Industries, such as breweries and the animal-feed merchants FE Stevens, were stalwart users of the canal for transporting their produce. Today, many of the original warehouses have survived, these days serving new purposes. Prominent among these is the Clock Warehouse, formerly a corn mill. It is now a popular pub and restaurant where, in the summer months, customers sit outside and eat beneath shady willow trees. The old Salt Warehouse has become an antiques centre and its neighbour, Shardlow Heritage Centre,

The old Salt Warehouse at Shardlow.

gives visitors an insight to the history of Shardlow. Shardlow also has a long-established boatyard that can supply most boaters' needs; reaching the nearest shop involves a bit of a walk.

Further along the canal there are two old pubs standing side by side: the Malt Shovel and the New Inn. In the port's working heyday, its workers would have been well lubricated, as there were 14 pubs and three breweries in the town.

Leaving Shardlow, the canal follows the valley of the River Trent to Weston-on-Trent, where there is a lock and a village. Weston Lock is normally a very peaceful place, except when there is a meeting at Donington Park motor-racing circuit, which is less than a mile away from the canal.

Boating at Weston-on-Trent.

After the lock there is a beautiful wooded section called Weston Cliffs, which is close to a former Ukrainian settlement. This camp, known as Tarasivka, was set up at Weston-on-Trent after the Second World War as the home for the Ukrainian Youth Association in the UK.

Swarkestone is the junction with the former Derby Canal, which was abandoned in 1964. The 14-mile-long canal connected the Trent & Mersey Canal to the Erewash Canal at Sandiacre, and has an active restoration group. At present, the only navigable bit is by the entrance and is used for moorings by a boat club. Swarkestone Bridge over the Trent marks the southernmost point reached by Bonnie Prince Charlie on his march to London to claim the throne in 1745.

After a pleasant three miles of undulating countryside you arrive at the deep Stenson Lock, which has a tea room in the former lock cottage. Stenson Lock is the last wide lock until the canal reaches Middlewich. It also has a large marina, a boatyard and a pub.

Further along comes Mercia Marina, which is even bigger than Stenson Marina. It opened in 2008 and as well as nearly 600 berths for boats, it has a cafe, shop and holiday park with lodges. This is followed by Willington, with a landscaped area by its moorings, three convenient pubs and shops in the nearby town.

The busy A38 trunk road accompanies the canal between Willington and Burton upon Trent, where the one point of interest is in crossing Brindley's low aqueduct over the River Dove.

Burton upon Trent became famous as the world's number one brewery town. In 1880 it had 30 independent breweries, but because of mergers and closures there are only a few left today.

You can learn about the history of brewing at the National Brewery Centre museum, close to the town centre. For boaters, Horninglow Basin is a good stopping place for visiting the town, although the noise of the A38 road

ABOVE **Aqueduct over the River Dove.**

BELOW **Stenson Lock.**

overlooking the basin could be off-putting for those wanting to stay overnight.

Dallow Lane, the first narrow-gauge lock on the canal, is followed by Shobnall Basin where there is a boatyard with a hire fleet. Shobnall was the junction with the Bond End Canal that once connected the Trent & Mersey Canal to the River Trent. Disputes between the owners of the two canals meant that the Bond End Canal was never a success. Two of the remaining big breweries are close to Shobnall Basin; this will soon be apparent as you get a waft of malt and hops as you pass by.

Horninglow Basin at Burton upon Trent.

Burton upon Trent to Fradley Junction

Leaving Burton upon Trent, the canal heads out into the countryside to Branston, which gave its name to the pickle that was once manufactured in the village. This is a beautiful section with a pretty lock and bridge at Tatenhill. Here there is a popular canalside pub called The Bridge as well as Branston Water Park, a large lake that was created from disused gravel workings and which is now a nature reserve. There is a visitor centre and there are many footpaths around the site.

The A38 trunk road has never been far away, but now at Barton-under- Needwood it is almost on the towpath. Barton Marina has lots of shops, a gallery, pub, cafes and restaurants as well as a 300-berth marina. The canal and the A38 thankfully part company at Wychnor and the canal then goes on to Alrewas. Boaters should be aware of the large weir, where the River Trent comes in and joins the canal for a

The lake at Branston Water Park.

The National Memorial Arboretum

The Arboretum opened in 1997 and is set in 150 acres of beautiful woodland and gardens. It has over 200 memorials honouring 16,000 armed services personnel who have died in various conflicts since the end of the Second World War. The Arboretum is also home to 50,000 trees, with more added each year, and the visitor centre has a restaurant and several shops. From Alrewas village it is a 15-minute walk, or alternatively there is a bus service to the Arboretum.

One of the displays at the National Memorial Arboretum.

short distance. Alrewas village has plenty of shops and pubs, and is the nearest point from which to visit the National Memorial Arboretum.

Fradley Junction is where the Coventry Canal joins the Trent & Mersey Canal. Geographically it is a remote spot on the map, but in reality it is often a very busy place crammed with boats and visitors who come by car to visit the Fradley Pool Nature Reserve and watch the boats pass down five locks. A former British Waterways maintenance yard bedecked with a redundant crane is now a cafe and information centre, and a two-storey warehouse contains an art gallery with a bookshop. Nearby is a holiday park with a cafe, an indoor swimming pool and tennis courts for holiday hirers. This complex is set away from the canal, but the cafe is open to the passing public. The 200-year-old Swan Inn faces the junction with the Coventry Canal and this is where we turn left on the next stage of the journey.

Fradley Junction.

practical information

Distance: Shardlow to Fradley is 26 miles with 17 locks.

Boaters: The first six locks on the journey are broad gauge and the rest narrow.

Walkers: There is a continuous path throughout and no tunnels. There is a railway station at Burton-on-Trent but no other rail connections on this stretch of canal.

Places of interest: Shardlow's old inland port, and the National Brewery Centre museum at Burton upon Trent.

Key pubs: Clock Warehouse at Shardlow; The Malt Shovel at Shardlow; The Bridge at Branston; and The Swan at Fradley Junction.

Canal footbridge over the River Trent at Alrewas.

Chapter 15

The Coventry Canal at Hartshill.

COVENTRY CANAL

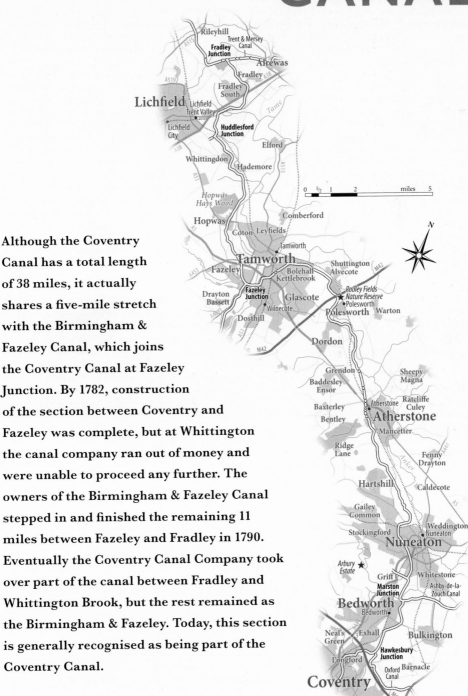

Although the Coventry Canal has a total length of 38 miles, it actually shares a five-mile stretch with the Birmingham & Fazeley Canal, which joins the Coventry Canal at Fazeley Junction. By 1782, construction of the section between Coventry and Fazeley was complete, but at Whittington the canal company ran out of money and were unable to proceed any further. The owners of the Birmingham & Fazeley Canal stepped in and finished the remaining 11 miles between Fazeley and Fradley in 1790. Eventually the Coventry Canal Company took over part of the canal between Fradley and Whittington Brook, but the rest remained as the Birmingham & Fazeley. Today, this section is generally recognised as being part of the Coventry Canal.

The weathered junction stone between the Coventry Canal and Birmingham & Fazeley Canal at Whittington Brook.

The Coventry Canal was an integral part of engineer James Brindley's plan to link the River Trent with the Thames at Oxford, following a course through the Warwickshire coalfields. It was coal that made the canal prosperous, with the bulk of the product at first being carried on the Oxford Canal then later on the Grand Union Canal to London and the south. Most of the mines serviced by the canal have since closed, but in some cases the entries to their loading basins can still be seen. Despite its industrial past, much of the Coventry Canal now presents a green and pastoral aspect to the visiting boater. There are only 13 locks and 11 of these are grouped together at Atherstone.

Fradley Junction to Fazeley

Leaving the Trent & Mersey Canal at Fradley Junction, the Coventry Canal passes an industrial centre built on the site of an old airfield. It then takes a twisting southerly course to Streethay Wharf where you can take a bus to the cathedral city of Lichfield, only two miles away. At Huddlesford there is a waterside pub called The Plough Inn near to the junction with the Lichfield Canal. The first section is used by the Lichfield Cruising Club for moorings, but after that it is derelict. As an extension of the Wyrley & Essington Canal, it once formed a vital connection between the Black Country canals and the Coventry Canal but was abandoned in 1954 and filled in in several places. There is a vigorous campaign to restore the canal, led by the Lichfield & Hatherton Canal Restoration Trust. A new aqueduct constructed over the M6 toll motorway stands unconnected and without water at present, awaiting the day when boats return to the canal.

Next comes Whittington village, which has a waterside pub called The Swan that is a pleasant place to stop for a

Hopwas Hays Wood.

while. Look out for the boundary stone that divided the Coventry Canal and the Birmingham & Fazeley Canal. The Coventry Canal is now following the River Tame valley and the next section at Hopwas Hays Wood is probably the prettiest on its entire length. This lovely stretch of waterway has the river on one side and a forest on the other. Exploration of Hopwas Hays Wood needs some care as part of it is used as a firing range, but notices are posted when this is in progress. Hopwas village has two pubs facing each other across the water, which makes it a tempting place to linger awhile.

The Birmingham & Fazeley Canal begins its journey in central Birmingham and ends at Fazeley Junction where it joins the Coventry Canal. The junction is surrounded by roads, but although it's a bit noisy it is worth stopping to look at the architecture. It has two fine mill buildings, one of which was built in 1790 by Sir Robert Peel, father of the Prime Minister of the same name. There is also a junction house, and the Canal & River Trust has its offices and yard at Peel's Wharf next to the junction.

Fazeley Junction.

Fazeley to Hawkesbury Junction

After leaving Fazeley, the canal crosses the River Tame on a substantial aqueduct. This is closely followed by two locks at Glascote, where the main feature is a large boatyard with a dry dock set in its own basin. Here you are very near the centre of Tamworth, and you can reach it with an easy walk from the bridge above the locks. Tamworth has a Norman castle with well-preserved motte-and-bailey architecture, once painted by the artist JMW Turner.

The next part of the journey is very built-up as the canal passes through Amington, a suburb of Tamworth. At the edge of Amington, you come to Alvecote Marina with the Samuel Barlow pub, which is named after a well-known fleet of canal carriers and overlooks the canal.

The ruins of the 12th-century Alvecote Priory can be seen close to the Marina. The main entrance arch is the remaining feature of the former Benedictine monastery.

A Samuel Barlow boat moored outside the company's namesake pub at Alvecote Marina.

Samuel Barlow

Samuel Barlow, the son of a boatman, started his business in 1867 carrying coal from the local mines by the Coventry Canal. In 1870 he moved to Glascote and with ten boats began carrying coal over long distances from the Tamworth area to London and the River Thames. He died suddenly in 1894 aged 47, but his two sons carried on the business. By 1930 the fleet had expanded to 70 boats and the company had moved its headquarters to Birmingham. Trade declined after the Second World War and the company ceased trading in 1962. Barlow's boats had a reputation for the fine, detailed artwork used to decorate their cabins, a tradition that continued to the very end.

A pair of Samuel Barlow boats loaded with coal on the Coventry Canal in 1958.

From Alvecote Priory there is a trail to Alvecote Pools, a nature reserve created by mining subsidence. The trail, once used by miners, allows visitors to see wading birds from a tree-fringed footpath. After Alvecote comes Pooley Fields Nature Reserve, also created as a result of mining subsidence. Here, spoil heaps from Pooley Hall Colliery have been grassed over, providing views around the site. The canal passes through a wooded cutting by Pooley Hall Manor house and then enters Polesworth.

Coal mining, quarrying and potteries made Polesworth a prosperous town during the 19th century. The canal played its part in transporting this produce, especially coal, which in the 1960s was still being carried by water from Pooley Hall Colliery. The canal then passes through the centre of the town, which is a good stopping place for shops, pubs and takeaways.

After Polesworth there is a three-mile stretch of open farming countryside before the Atherstone Flight of 11 locks at Bradley Green. The first six locks are set in countryside, with the final five being inside the town. Atherstone has been a centre for hat-making since the 17th century and once employed 3,000 people in its millinery factories. It is also known for its Shrove Tuesday ball game, which has been played in the town's streets since the 12th century. There are

no goals and the only rule seems to be that players are not allowed to kill each other! Local shopkeepers usually board up their windows on that day… Just above the top lock is Rothen's coal yard, which still retains a feeling of yesteryear, when the yard was busy loading boats with coal to take to London and the south.

The canal continues on its southerly course to Hartshill, where at the maintenance yard there is a superb collection of mid-19th century buildings. These were once the Coventry Canal Company workshops, and are occupied today by the Canal & River Trust's maintenance yard and offices. The centrepiece is an arched dock topped by an elegant clock tower. Other notable structures include a stable block, a blacksmith's shop and the manager's house.

Between Hartshill and Nuneaton the ground is made up of layers of slate and shale. The presence of these resources led to extensive quarrying for road building and railway ballast, and the stone was carried to London and Birmingham by canal boat. Conical spoil heaps are now

OPPOSITE **The entrance arch of the ruined Alvecote Priory.**

ABOVE **The Coventry Canal passing by the Pooley Fields Nature Reserve.**

BELOW **Rothen's coal yard at Atherstone in 1984.**

covered in shrubs and grass and are sometimes jovially called 'alps' by the local population. One of these is prominent as you leave Hartshill. It's a beautiful section, and it is hard to believe that it was once a hive of industry with several quarries on its banks.

Nuneaton is unlikely to be awarded any gold stars by VisitEngland. The canal passes through a seemingly endless procession of houses with the occasional break for playing fields. Nuneaton has plenty of shops and pubs, but few of them are by the water. In contrast, the Arbury Estate on the outskirts of Nuneaton is surrounded by beautiful landscaped gardens, and Arbury Hall was the birthplace of Victorian novelist Mary Anne Evans, better known by her pen name George Eliot. The estate has been in the hands of the Newdigate family since 1586, and one of the more energetic owners was Sir Roger Newdigate. He inherited the estate in 1734 at the age of 14, and went on to build a system of private

Hartshill maintenance yard.

canals connected by tramroads to carry coal and other produce from Arbury to the Coventry Canal between 1764 and 1790. The entire system was six miles long and had several locks, but closed after his death in 1806.

Nearby Griff Hollows Canal was another waterway, built to connect the Coventry Canal to the Griff Colliery, just south of Nuneaton. This stayed in use until the mine closed in 1961, and its entrance can still be seen. Marston Junction marks the start of the Ashby Canal, and is very close to the point where the Arbury Canal met the Coventry Canal. The Ashby Canal offers 22 miles of lock-free cruising through mainly rural countryside, and is popular with boaters.

Just beyond Marston Junction is a boatyard called Charity Dock, which usually displays a vintage collection of old narrowboats. Then, at the end of a wooded cutting, you can see the entrance to the Newdigate Colliery Arm that closed in 1982. Most of the coal carried by boat from Newdigate

The canal at Hartshill with one of the 'Hartshill alps' in the background.

Joe Skinner

One notable Hawkesbury character was Joe Skinner, who was known as 'the last of the Number Ones'. The 'Number Ones' were a group of owner boatmen who preferred to work with horses and mules in the traditional manner rather than use motor transport. Joe was born in 1893 into a boating family and spent all his life on the canals. He married Rose and for years they delivered coal from the Warwickshire coalfields to Oxford. They worked with the boat *Friendship*, which stayed in their possession for the rest of their lives and now is restored as an exhibit in the National Waterways Museum at Ellesmere Port. Joe died in 1975 aged 82, and Rose the following year aged 77.

ABOVE Joe and Rose Skinner in retirement on their boat *Friendship* at Hawkesbury in 1974.

RIGHT The restored *Friendship* as an exhibit in the National Waterways Museum at Ellesmere Port.

and Griff Collieries went south, either to London or to the paper mills at Hemel Hempstead. At this point the canal passes by the old mining town of Bedworth, but it requires a longish walk to reach the town centre.

Our journey has now reached Hawkesbury, which marks the junction with the Oxford Canal. A splendid cast-iron junction bridge faces a boatman's pub and there is an engine house that once supplied the Coventry Canal with water from a Newcomen steam engine. When its working days were over, the engine went to a museum in Dartmouth but the engine house is still there, surrounded by modern buildings.

The junction became a meeting place for boating people waiting for orders to load from nearby collieries. The working boat people called the junction Sutton Stop after the Sutton family of 19th-century lock-keepers.

The route as described in this book leaves the Coventry Canal at Hawkesbury and joins the Oxford Canal. But before leaving the junction boaters may consider completing the final five miles of the Coventry Canal into the city of Coventry. Walkers should be able to catch a bus from Longford Bridge, about a mile from the junction, and an art trail then takes the canal into Coventry Basin, where there are moorings and a sculpture of James Brindley. From there it is a short walk to the cathedral and city-centre shops.

practical information

Distance: Fradley Junction to Hawkesbury Junction is 38 miles with 13 narrow locks.

Boaters: No special instructions.

Walkers: There is a continuous towpath and there are no tunnels. There are railway stations near the canal at Tamworth, Polesworth, Atherstone and Bedworth. The station at Nuneaton is a longer walk away from the canal.

Places of interest: Pooley Fields Nature Reserve and Arbury Estate, the birthplace of George Eliot.

Key pubs: Canalside pubs occur at regular intervals, with two facing each other across the canal at Hopwas.

A working pair of narrowboats at Hawkesbury resting before continuing their journey south with coal from Atherstone.

Chapter 16

Newbold Tunnel near Rugby.

OXFORD CANAL

The Oxford Canal, initially designed and engineered by James Brindley, was part of his Grand Cross of canals linking the major rivers – in this case the Trent and the Thames. Although construction began in 1769, it took another 21 years to complete the waterway to Oxford, by which time Brindley had died. Apart from being an important long-distance link, it enabled coal from the Warwickshire coalfields to be brought south to Banbury, Oxford and the Thames via the Coventry Canal.

Bedworth
Bedworth
Bulkington
Exhall
Neal's Green
Hawkesbury Junction
Barnacle
The Greyhound Inn
Shilton
Pongford
Coventry Canal
Ansty
Coventry
Foleshill
Pailton
Stretton under Fosse
Brinklow
Easenhall
Harborough Magna
Bretford
Avon
Brownsover
Clifton upon Dunsmore
King's Newham
Little Lawford
Newbold on Avon
Avon Aqueduct
Rugby
Webb Ellis Rugby Football Museum
Hilmorton
Dunchurch
Kilsby
Barby
Woolscott
Willoughby
Grandborough
Braunston Turn
Braunston
Stockton Locks
Grand Union Canal
Sawbridge
Grand Union Canal
Braunston Tunnel
Stockton
Calcutt Locks
Nethercote
Southam
Napton Junction
Lower Shuckburgh
Napton on the Hill
The Folly
Ladbroke
Marston Doles
Priors Marston
Priors Hardwick
Knightcote
Wormleighton
Upper Boddington
The Wharf Inn
Fenny Compton
Lower Boddington
Aston le Walls
Farnborough
Claydon
Chipping Warden
Farnborough
Upper Wardington
The Red Lion
Cropredy
Williamscot
Great Bourton
Hanwell
Chacombe
Banbury Museum
Tooley's Boatyard
Banbury
Banbury

Oxford Canal

Hawkesbury Junction to Banbury...

N

0 ½ 1 2 miles 5

Map continues on page 204.

Physically, the Oxford Canal is a typical Brindley waterway, winding around the contours and only resorting to locks when there was no alternative way of avoiding higher ground. Today, this method of canal construction is very appealing for pleasure boating, but it was an anathema for working boatmen who had schedules to meet. The monopoly on trade to the south lasted just 15 years before the Grand Junction Canal opened with a more direct route and wider locks between Braunston and London. Revenues on the Oxford Canal plunged, something drastic had to be done and in 1829 the Oxford Canal Company began straightening out the section between Hawkesbury and Braunston. The old meandering curves were replaced by deep cuttings and embankments, reducing the original journey by 15 miles. Most of the old loops and branches are now derelict but some remain in water and are used for mooring.

The 75-mile-long Oxford Canal is a delight for both boaters and walkers who will find the towpath designated as a long-distance footpath. Apart from the towns of Rugby and Banbury, the canal passes through remote countryside amid some of the finest scenery in Warwickshire and Oxfordshire.

Oxford Canal near Napton Junction.

Hawkesbury Junction to Rugby

After leaving Hawkesbury Junction, the first two miles of the Oxford Canal are overshadowed by motorways. The Coventry Cruising Club has its moorings on an old colliery arm that is directly beneath the M6.

Some relief comes at the village of Ansty, which has a canalside pub called The Rose & Castle, named after the rose and castle motifs often used by the working boatmen when decorating their boats in colourful style.

At Nettle Hill the railway comes very close to the canal, which then disappears into a deep wooded cutting, making it invisible from the trackside.

The canal and railway remain close neighbours for another two miles to Stretton Stop, where they part company. The boatyard at Stretton Stop has all boating facilities plus a hire fleet, boat building, provisions shop and chandlery. The old arm to Stretton Wharf is now used for moorings. A handsome cast-iron towpath bridge marks the entrance to the former Brinklow Arm that once led into the centre of Brinklow village, until it became one of the casualties of the

ABOVE **Wooded cutting at Nettle Hill.**

BELOW **A rose and castle motif on a narrowboat cabin door.**

canal being straightened out in 1829. The cast-iron towpath bridge is an excellent example of a Horseley Ironworks bridge, which can be seen throughout the Midlands canals. Look out for the rope grooving on the top of the bridge, caused by chafing towropes from generations of horse-drawn working boats.

For the next few miles the canal passes through lovely wooded countryside to Cathiron, where the old Fennis Field Arm leads into a large new marina. A wooded cutting continues to Newbold Tunnel, which was built in the 1830s, replacing the original structure whose entrance can still be seen behind the church in the village. The present tunnel has a towpath and its interior has been illuminated with garish lighting.

Boaters and walkers wishing to recover from the lighting display will find two pubs at the end of the tunnel. You then enter the suburbs of Rugby, where there is a mixture of industrial estates and housing next to the canal. Rugby is famous for its public school, where William Webb Ellis picked up a soccer ball and ran with it, thereby inventing a new form of football. There are various museums in the town dedicated to the school and the sport.

For boaters wishing to stock up on provisions there is a large supermarket and retail centre near a little park at Brownsover, and there is a canalside pub next to the weeded-up Brownsover Arm. The navigable Rugby Wharf Arm is almost opposite with its entrance spanned by another fine Horseley Ironworks bridge. The arm is now used for moorings and has a boatyard.

The canal continues to Clifton Upon Dunsmore where there is a boatyard with all boating facilities and a hire fleet. One more mile takes the canal to Hillmorton where, in an attractive setting, there are three duplicated locks and the lockside cafe called Canalchef Cafe. A short arm by Granthams Bridge once led to the Canal Company workshops, and this is now the Hillmorton Locks Canal Centre with boat services and a repair yard.

The Webb Ellis Rugby Football Museum.

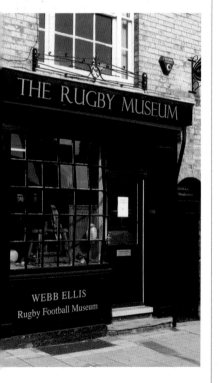

LEFT **Granthams Bridge leading to the Hillmorton Locks Canal Centre.**

BELOW **Horseley Ironworks towpath bridge over the entrance to the Brinklow Arm.**

BOTTOM **The interior of Newbold Tunnel.**

Rugby to Napton

Leaving Hillmorton Locks, the landscape to the east is dominated by the masts of Rugby Radio Station. At Wharf Bridge there is the Old Royal Oak, a large pub with a restaurant, and after that the canal heads out into open countryside. Uneven bumps and patterns in some fields are remnants of a medieval method of farming known as 'ridge and furrow'. This was the result of ploughing with non-reversible ploughs on the same strip of land year after year. It is visible on land ploughed in the Middle Ages but has not been used since. The M45 motorway disturbs the peace for a short while, but after that it is tranquillity all the way to Braunston.

The northern section of the Oxford Canal ends at Braunston, where it shares the waterway with the Grand Union Canal for five miles. The Oxford Canal skirts around the edge of the village before passing beneath the elegant double-arched junction bridge that marks the conjoining of the two waterways.

The double-arched junction bridge at Braunston.

Napton to Fenny Compton

You bid farewell to the Grand Union Canal at Napton
Junction and continue the journey on the South Oxford
Canal. Opposite the junction is a large marina called
Wigrams Turn, the name used by the working boatmen for
Napton Junction. Another marina and a pub soon follow, and
then the canal begins to wind around Napton Hill.

The shortening of the North Oxford Canal did not
happen south of Napton and for that today's boaters and

Descending Napton Locks.

Mikron Theatre Company

The Mikron Theatre Company was founded in 1963 by the actor Mike Lucas. Since 1971 they have travelled the English waterways on their narrowboat *Tysley* performing at pubs, village halls and boating festivals during the summer months. The company is based at Marsden in Yorkshire by the Huddersfield Narrow Canal. It relies on sponsorship and takings on the day of the performance to pay its wages and fuel costs.

TOP RIGHT Mikron Theatre Company on their boat *Tysley* in 1993. The founder Mike Lucas is at the tiller next to his late wife Sarah. Members of the cast are Richard Povall and Becky Hall (standing) with Sarah Parks and Rodney Matthew (sitting down).

BOTTOM RIGHT The 1993 cast performing *Imogen's War* at Fenny Compton, including Richard Povall, Lucy McAra, Becky Hall and Rodney Matthew.

walkers should be eternally grateful. Brindley's canal remains as it was built in the 1770s, following the contours around beautiful hillsides (such as the one at Napton). There are nine locks on the Napton flight, with the first six being close together. Looking back from the bottom lock you have a fine view of Napton Hill topped by a windmill. Before tackling the first lock, consider a walk along the lane to Napton village or visit the pub along the track by the lock. This pub, now called The Folly, was once a favourite inn of the working boatmen called The Bull and Butcher. An evocative description of the pub as it was in 1939 can be found in LTC Rolt's classic book *Narrow Boat*.

After Atkins Lock, the entrance to the Old Engine House Arm can be seen. Now used for moorings, this arm once led to a building that housed a steam engine pumping water back to the canal's summit level through a brick channel. The later construction of Boddington Reservoir made the engine redundant. At Marston Doles top lock there is a cluster of buildings with cottages, stables and an old warehouse.

Once past the lock, you are on the canal's summit level with 11 miles of winding waterway through gloriously remote countryside. At first you come to a series of bewildering convolutions known as the Wormleighton Loops. Wormleighton is a village surrounded by hills and the canal almost completes a full circle as it passes around Wormleighton Hill, often causing boaters and walkers to lose all sense of direction. In the summertime the canal banks take on all the colours of an artist's palette, with myriad wild flowers. Look up and you may be lucky to see a red kite hovering overhead. The towpath can be a bit overgrown in the summertime, making walking difficult after wet weather. The last pub was nine miles back at Napton Top Lock, but at last refreshment appears at Fenny Compton where there is The Wharf Inn, some basic boating facilities and then a marina. Next comes Fenny Compton cutting. This was once a tunnel but it was opened out in the 1860s when landslips threatened to collapse the roof.

Steam driven narrowboat at Napton.

Fenny Compton to Banbury

After Fenny Compton we pass Wormleighton Reservoir, whose waters now feed the summit level that ends at Claydon Top Lock. The group of buildings by the top lock were once maintenance workshops and stables. The five locks at Claydon are beautifully situated in open countryside, and Claydon village itself is half a mile away from the third lock down. Accessing shops and pubs is much easier at Cropredy, the next village on the canal. There's the thatched The Red Lion pub close to Cropredy Lock, and a general store by the bridge. Cropredy was the location for a Civil War battle in 1644, and there are some weapons on display in the church. These days, the village is more famous for its annual Fairport Convention music festival that brings thousands of visitors into the village every August.

OPPOSITE TOP **Lift bridge in the centre of Banbury.**

BELOW **Cropredy Lock.**

Banbury is the largest town on the Oxford Canal before you reach the city of Oxford itself. The canal passes an industrial area and then under the M40 motorway bridge

before reaching the town centre and the Castle Quay Shopping Centre, with all the usual high-street shops undercover. Banbury Museum, which is connected to the shopping area, has its own bridge over the canal. Adjoining the museum is Tooley's Boatyard, the only surviving boatyard in continuous use on a narrow canal, and where LTC Rolt began his epic journey around the canals in 1939.

Next to the canal there is also an arts centre and an attractive park. One of the interesting features of the canal between Banbury and Oxford is its lift bridges, and there is one to negotiate by Tooley's Boatyard before entering Banbury Lock.

LTC Rolt

In July 1939, author Tom Rolt and his wife Angela left Banbury on a 400-mile cruise around Britain's decaying canals on their boat *Cressy*, which had been refitted at Tooley's Boatyard. The cruise led to Tom writing his classic book *Narrow Boat*, describing their journey and the places and people they met in the last months before the Second World War. Published in 1944, the book inspired Robert Aickman, Charles Hadfield and Tom Rolt to set up the Inland Waterways Association in 1946, which has successfully campaigned for the restoration and preservation of Britain's inland waterways. There is a memorial plaque on the Tom Rolt Bridge near Banbury shopping centre.

LEFT **Tooley's Boatyard at Banbury.**

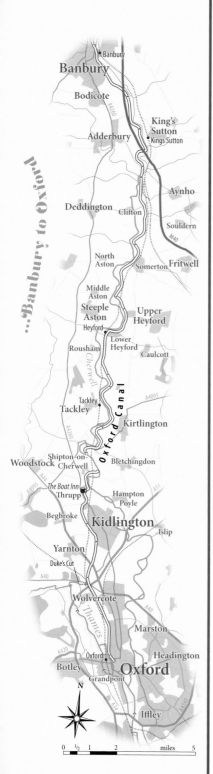

...Banbury to Oxford

Banbury to Oxford

Urban Banbury lingers awhile as the canal leaves the town and heads southwards. Lift bridges appear frequently on this stretch, but fortunately many of them are chained open in the lifted position. There is another encounter with the M40 motorway before the canal reaches King's Sutton Lock, and soon afterwards the motorway crosses the canal for the last time, leaving the canal to follow its peaceful course southwards along the valley of the River Cherwell.

At Nell Bridge Lock, the towpath disappears, so walkers have to cross a busy main road to regain the path on the other side, leading to Aynho Weir Lock. This lock is fed by water from the River Cherwell, which enters the canal above the lock on the same level. A long line of moorings leads to Aynho Wharf, where there is a pub and a boatyard with all facilities.

Aynho Weir Lock is an unusual diamond shape, which allows an increase in the volume of water in order to balance the Somerton Deep Lock that follows (at 12 feet deep, Somerton Deep Lock has the distinction of being one of the deepest narrow locks on the entire system). Shipton Weir Lock further along the canal has a similar shape for the same reason.

At Somerton the canal, river and railway all squeeze together in close proximity, sharing the lovely Cherwell Valley. There was a time when the tranquil section between Somerton and the Heyfords was subjected to screaming low-flying jet planes from the United States Air Force base at Upper Heyford. Now the base has closed the only disturbance to the peace comes from the trains passing along the valley. A busy boatyard at Lower Heyford, with all facilities and a hire fleet, faces Heyford Station, which is so close it is almost on the towpath.

ABOVE **Summertime boating at Somerton.**

OPPOSITE **Oxford Canal near King's Sutton.**

ABOVE **Idyllic boating near Lower Heyford.**

BELOW **Isis Lock, near the end of the canal in Oxford.**

The next five miles below Lower Heyford are some of the most beautiful and remote on the English waterway system. Wooded hills close in on the canal, sometimes forming tunnels of greenery, and the river can usually be seen beside the towpath. This is an area rich in wildlife, with running water from the river attracting all types of birds. There was once a boatman's pub by the remote Pigeon Lock but it closed years ago. Tackley village is quite close at one point but the wooded hillsides make it invisible from the canal. No road bridge intrudes until you reach Enslow, where The Rock of Gibraltar pub has a waterside garden.

After Baker's Lock, the River Cherwell joins the canal for about a mile. Boaters should be aware of a series of sharp bends and the possibility of the river flooding after heavy rain. A tall chimney belonging to a hidden cement works looks rather incongruous poking above the trees in this idyllic setting. Canal and river go their separate ways after the diamond-shaped Shipton Weir Lock.

The next section of the canal achieved some notoriety on Christmas Eve 1874 when a derailed train plunged into the canal, killing 34 passengers and injuring 69. This occured close to Shipton-on-Cherwell, a charming village with a waterside church. The canal takes a sharp right-hand turn under a lift bridge at Thrupp. Here, there are facilities for boaters and in a former maintenance yard a group of mellow buildings contains a tea room. Beyond the bridge, a row of old cottages faces the canal. Moorings and The Boat Inn – the first waterside pub since Enslow three miles away – make Thrupp a pleasant place to linger awhile.

Two more pubs follow in quick succession, although both share the canal with a main road. The canal then skirts around the houses and industrial estates of Kidlington, which is really a dormitory suburb of Oxford. There is not a lot to see here apart from the shops, which are probably best reached from Bridge.

At Duke's Cut on the outskirts of Oxford, boaters are faced with a choice: either turn on to the Duke's Cut and join the River Thames above Godstow thus avoiding the canal in Oxford, or carry on through Wolvercote, with its pub on the village green. Either way, you will find yourself entering the fair city of Oxford by the 'back door'. You will see no colleges or dreaming spires on the approach – that will come later. Although there is some industry, you mostly pass houses with gardens and modern apartment blocks, such as the converted former Lucy's Eagle Ironworks. The terraced streets of Jericho, often used as a location in the Inspector Morse TV series, show another side of old working-class Oxford.

A fine cast-iron footbridge in front of Isis Lock takes you along the final stretch of the canal now used for moorings. Isis Lock itself provides the exit into the Thames via a series of backwaters and a railway bridge. The canal once terminated at a basin near Oxford Castle but this was filled in to create a car park for Nuffield College. Now a raised circular plaque marks the end of the Oxford Canal at Hythe Bridge. Turn left here for the city centre.

practical information

Distance: The total distance between Hawkesbury Junction and the River Thames at Oxford is 75 miles with 46 narrow locks and 1 tunnel at Newbold.

Boaters: Take care after heavy rain on the section shared by the canal and River Cherwell.

Walkers: The towpath is continuous and designated as a long-distance footpath. Oxford's station is close to the end of the canal and from there you can reach Tackley, Lower Heyford, King's Sutton and Banbury, all of which have stations near the canal. Above Banbury the canal becomes very remote and there are no railway connections.

Places of interest: Banbury Museum; Tooley's Boatyard at Banbury; and Webb Ellis Rugby Football Museum.

Key pubs: The Greyhound Inn at Hawkesbury Junction; The Folly at Napton; The Wharf Inn at Fenny Compton; The Red Lion at Cropredy; Two pubs at Thrupp; and Rock of Gibralter at Enslow.

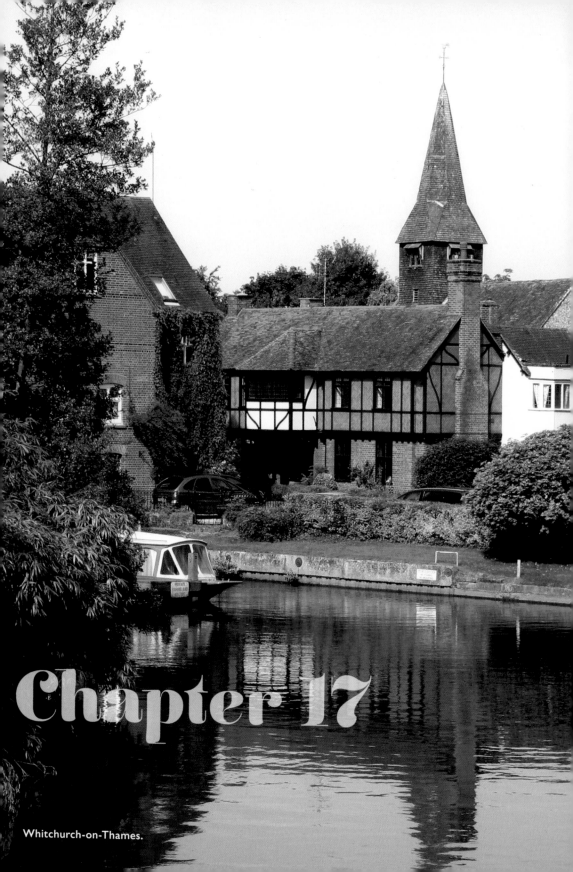

Chapter 17

Whitchurch-on-Thames.

RIVER THAMES

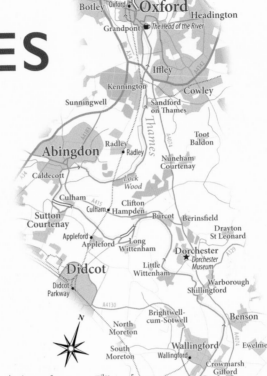

The 42-mile section of the River Thames between Oxford and Reading passes through ancient towns such as Abingdon-on-Thames and Wallingford and has some of the finest scenery on the entire river. The stretch between Goring and Pangbourne is outstanding in its natural beauty and is equally matched by the section between Sandford-on-Thames and Abingdon. It is hard to imagine this part of the Thames once being a busy commercial river but, until the Grand Junction Canal was built, this was the only inland water connection between London and the Midlands via the Oxford Canal.

Oxford to Iffley

Boaters leave the Oxford Canal at Isis Lock, which leads them into a backwater of the Thames called Sheepwash Channel. Follow this stream into the Thames just before Osney Bridge, watching out for the low headroom (7 feet 6 inches). This is unlikely to affect craft leaving the Oxford Canal but it does restrict those large river cruisers often referred to as 'gin palaces' from reaching the Upper Thames. Walkers have two options: they can follow the canal towpath to its end at Hythe Bridge and then turn right to reach Osney Bridge, or a more attractive alternative is to continue onwards, follow the Castle Mill Stream past Oxford Castle to the Thames, and cross the river on a footbridge below Osney Rail Bridge.

Old industrial buildings near Osney Bridge, Oxford.

The attractions of Oxford are many despite the fact that the city does not always show its best face to the river. Until recent times Oxford's waterside was largely industrial, but now most of the factories and foundries that lined the banks have closed. These have been replaced by housing with riverside views that must send local estate agents singing all the way to the bank.

Folly Bridge is a good place to stop and explore the city. Next to it, there is an eccentric castellated building covered in flint and statues, and there is also the large waterside The Head of the River pub, with a garden. Salter's Steamers boat services have a base here.

Folly Bridge road runs into St Aldates, leading into the city centre. As well as the covered market and shopping arcades there is much to see, including the Carfax Tower, Radcliffe Camera, Sheldonian Theatre, Ashmolean Museum and several other museums. There are 38 colleges in Oxford

ABOVE **The Radcliffe Camera in Oxford.**

BELOW **The River Cherwell at Christ Church Meadow.**

and most of them are open to the public at selected times. Oxford University has 22,000 students and some of them can be seen jogging on the Thames towpath or out on the water rowing when they are not studying for their degrees. For a different take on the city, try one of the Inspector Morse conducted tours, visiting locations used in the popular television series.

Also by Folly Bridge is the riverside Christ Church Meadow, overlooked by Christ Church Cathedral. From the meadow you can follow the River Cherwell to the Botanic Gardens and Magdalen Bridge, where you can hire punts to potter about on the Cherwell.

Iffley to Abingdon-on-Thames

Iffley Lock is in an attractive setting and is one of the oldest locks on the river. Nearby Iffley village has a Norman church, and Iffley Meadows nature reserve is famous for thousands of fritillary flowers that bloom in the spring. The Isis Farmhouse is a waterside pub and cafe with a garden near the lock, but can only be reached on foot, bike or boat as there is no road access.

The Kings Arms is another popular waterside pub at Sandford, next to one of the deepest locks on the Thames. The infamous Sandford Lasher pool below the weir has no public access for health and safety reasons. Over the years many people have drowned here, including the 21-year-old Michael Llewelyn Davies, who was the foster son of JM Barrie and believed to be the writer's inspiration for Peter Pan.

The next four miles between Sandford and Abingdon are very pretty, with no road crossings and just one railway bridge. Wooded hills sweep down to the river at Nuneham Courtenay and by Radley College boathouse. Almost hidden by trees is Nuneham House and park, where the newlywed Queen Victoria and Prince Albert had a holiday in 1841. In her diary the Queen wrote: 'This is a most lovely place,' no doubt impressed with the park, which was designed by Capability Brown.

The river now bends to the west towards Abingdon Lock, passing the entrance to the Swift Ditch. In medieval times the river was diverted to feed water to a mill via the Swift Ditch but was returned to its natural course in the late 18th century; the Swift Ditch is now a muddy backwater. After leaving Abingdon Lock, the river bends southwards towards the town centre and Abingdon Bridge.

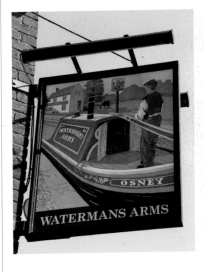

The Waterman's Arms near Osney Bridge.

Abingdon-on-Thames to Wallingford

Abingdon has a splendid waterfront dominated by St Helen's Church, whose spire rises above a row of old almshouses and a pub. Look for the 15th-century Abbey Gateway between Abingdon County Hall Museum and the Guildhall. Only a few ruins remain of the former Benedictine abbey but the Abbey Meadow is now a public park.

The cast-iron bridge at the junction with the River Ock was presented by the Wilts & Berks Canal Trust, which once had a junction at Abingdon. The Wilts & Berks Canal, which ran for 51 miles to join the Kennet & Avon Canal at Semington, closed in 1914 but there are ambitious plans to restore the waterway back to being a navigation. A new connection with the Thames (known as the Jubilee Junction) has now been created further downriver, by Abingdon Marina.

After the marina, the river bends very sharply to the east and enters the Culham Cut, leading to Culham Lock. The

Abingdon waterside, with St Helen's Church spire in the background.

natural river continues to Sutton Courtenay where the author George Orwell of Nineteen Eighty-Four fame is buried in the churchyard.

After Culham Lock, the navigation returns to the natural river as far as Clifton Cut, where another artificial channel leads to Clifton Hampden Bridge. The bridge was built by Sir George Gilbert Scott, who was also responsible for the Albert Memorial and St Pancras railway station in London. Nearby is the thatched Barley Mow pub, a favourite of Jerome K Jerome, who wrote part of *Three Men in a Boat* while staying there.

Below Clifton Lock is a backwater that is navigable to Long Wittenham, where there is The Plough Inn and the Pendon Museum, which is home to working model railways and a miniature landscape of the Vale of White Horse. The river then takes a wide bend for two miles before reaching Day's Lock, from where you get splendid views of the Sinodun Hills topped by Wittenham Clumps. A path from

TOP **Poppy field by the Culham Cut.**

ABOVE **Clifton Hampden Bridge, which opened in 1867.**

the lock crosses a footbridge that achieves fame once a year as the location for the World Pooh Sticks Championships.

Follow the path over the bridge towards Little Wittenham and a footpath on the left will take you to the top of Wittenham Clumps, where you will be rewarded with a splendid view of the river and Day's Lock. This area is a designated nature reserve run by the Earth Trust, and there is a visitor centre by a lane at the foot of the hill.

Another footpath from the lock will take you into the Roman town of Dorchester-on-Thames with its Norman abbey and a high street lined with a number of attractive old buildings. The Dorchester Abbey Tea Room is run by ladies from the village, with profits going to charities and towards the upkeep of the Abbey Museum.

Little Wittenham Bridge, the site of the annual World Pooh Sticks Championships.

After Day's Lock, the river bends sharply around Little Wittenham Wood to where the River Thames meets the smaller River Thame – very confusing nomenclature. Shillingford Bridge, the first road crossing over the river for five miles since Clifton Hampden, is overlooked by a large riverside hotel with an outdoor swimming pool. Next comes Benson Lock, which has a busy waterfront with boatyards, a caravan site and a riverside cafe. Beyond Benson Lock, the river passes the ruins of Wallingford Castle. The enormous Norman castle remained more or less intact until Cromwell destroyed it in 1652, but fragments can still be seen and it is well worth the trip before you enter Wallingford.

Wallingford to Pangbourne-on-Thames

Wallingford has a handsome town square overlooked by a 17th-century town hall, now a tourist information centre. Its many narrow streets are lined with shops, pubs and restaurants. The Cholsey and Wallingford Railway runs steam trains along a three-mile stretch.

After Wallingford, there are five miles of peaceful cruising uninterrupted by locks or road bridges. The only bridge to cross the water is Moulsford Railway Bridge, originally built by Brunel, but split into two parts when the bridge was widened. At Moulsford there is a diversion for walkers, where they have to leave the river and walk into the village before returning to the towpath. The Beetle & Wedge Boathouse pub and restaurant at Moulsford was immortalised as a location in Jerome K Jerome's novel *Three Men in a Boat*. This is followed by another classic riverside pub and restaurant

The ancient Wallingford Bridge has 17 arches, with five crossing the river.

Goring viewed from Streatley Hill.

called the Leatherne Bottel near Goring. This lovely open stretch of countryside ends at Cleeve Lock on the edge of Goring. The pound between Cleeve Lock and Goring Lock is only half a mile, making it the shortest on the river.

Goring-on-Thames and Streatley-on-Thames are twin villages facing each other across the river. Streatley is well known for its annual regatta and has a great view from the hill overlooking Goring and the river. Goring is larger, has more shops and the lock is wonderfully colourful in the summer. The wooded hills bordering the Goring Gap make it one of the finest cruising stretches on the entire river.

Just past Goring you will come to Beale Park – a wildlife park with a collection of exotic animals and birds. It stages an annual boat show, and has twice been the host for the Inland Waterways Association's National Festival and Boat Show. Behind Beale Park you should be able to see the 18th-century Palladian mansion Basildon Park. This has beautiful parkland and is now owned by the National Trust.

RIGHT **Boating on the Goring Gap near Beale Park.**

BELOW **Young canoeists and wildfowl share the river at Pangbourne Meadow with Whitchurch Bridge in the background.**

Walkers should follow the river on the Goring side, and once they are opposite Beale Park they will have to leave the towpath and follow a pretty footpath through woodland up to Whitchurch village, where they cross the toll bridge and return to the towpath at Pangbourne Meadow.

Pangbourne-on-Thames to Reading

Pangbourne is best known for being the home of Kenneth Grahame, author of *The Wind in the Willows*. Pangbourne Meadow, with its lovely backdrop of hills, is owned by the National Trust. In his book *Sweet Thames Run Softly*, published in 1940, Robert Gibbings described Pangbourne Meadow as, 'so crowded with views, they might have dropped from the gold frames of the Royal Academy.'

The river now reaches Mapledurham Lock, the first on the Thames to be mechanised, in 1956. The lock has an exquisite setting and in summer the lock garden is one of the most colourful on the river. It stands next to the Tudor Mapledurham House with its restored 15th-century mill still in working order. The house, believed to be the inspiration for Toad Hall in *The Wind in the Willows*, has been the location for many films including *The Forsyte Saga* television series and the 1976 film *The Eagle has Landed*.

The Reading Regatta at Thameside Promenade.

Swan Upping

Swan Upping takes place on the Thames over five days in July, between Sunbury and Abingdon. The crown retains the right to ownership of all unmarked mute swans, but on the Thames it shares this ownership with the Vintners and Dyers companies, who were granted rights in the 15th century. A group of skilled boatmen dressed in traditional costume row a colourfully decorated boat looking for unmarked cygnets, which are lifted on to the bank for tagging and health inspection. Although this is an historic ceremony dating from the 12th century, monitoring the numbers of swans annually enables suitable conservation methods to be used on the river.

The Swan Upping ceremony taking place at Reading.

After the lock there is once again a diversion away from the river for walkers. This time they must walk into Purley-on-Thames and rejoin the river below the marina. Purley and Tilehurst mark the outskirts of Reading, which looms in the distance. Tilehurst's railway station is very close to the riverside, where there is also a large boatyard and a supermarket.

The entry into Reading is pleasant, with housing and boathouses screened by trees on one side and open land on the other. Wide acres behind the Thameside Promenade and Little John's Farm are the site for Reading's annual music festival. The Reading Amateur Regatta is an annual event every June, and takes place over a one-mile-long course from St Mary's Island to Reading Rowing Club on the promenade near Caversham Bridge. The bridge uses an island in the

Caversham Bridge at Reading.

practical information

Distance: Between Oxford and Reading there are 42 miles of river with 11 manned locks.

Boaters: Boaters will need to have completed an Environment Agency short-period Thames licence, which is obtainable from the first Thames lock on the journey at Osney Lock.

Walkers: Walkers will find diversions at Shillingford; at Moulsford, between Goring-on-Thames and Whitchurch; and at Mapledurham. There are no railway stations near the river between Oxford and Goring, but there are stations at Goring-on-Thames, Pangbourne-on-Thames, Tilehurst and Reading.

Places of interest: Numerous attractions in Oxford and Abingdon; Dorchester Museum; Beale Park; and Mapledurham House.

Key pubs: A number of historic pubs and restaurants are en route including The Head of the River at Folly Bridge, Oxford; The Beetle & Wedge Boathouse at Moulsford; The Waterman's Arms near Osney Bridge in Oxford; and The Leatherne Bottel at Goring.

middle of the river as a central support, and is the first road crossing since the toll bridge at Whitchurch.

Fry's Island, situated between Caversham Bridge and Reading Bridge, has a bowling green and two boatyards with hire fleets, but can only be reached by ferry. Several passenger trip boats operate from the Caversham area, some of which are available for private hire. Caversham Lock is tucked away between an island and the wooded King's Meadow.

Reading's town centre is easily reached from either of the two Thames bridges but provisions can be obtained even more easily from a huge supermarket at the end of King's Meadow close to the start of the Kennet & Avon Canal.

ABOVE **Autumn colours at Reading's King's Meadow.**

Canoeists passing Hungerford Church.

Chapter 18

KENNET & AVON CANAL
EASTERN SECTION

The final part of our epic journey covers the 93 miles of the Kennet &
Avon Canal between Reading and Bristol Docks. The Kennet & Avon
Canal actually comprises three navigations: the River Kennet from
Reading to Newbury; the River Avon between Bath and Bristol; and
the 57-mile-long Kennet & Avon Canal that connects the two rivers.
The canal section contains a long flight of locks at Devizes and two
major aqueducts over the River Avon at Dundas and Avoncliff. The
river navigations were both navigable by the mid-18th century but the
canal took much longer to complete, mainly because of difficulties in
constructing the locks at Devizes. It was 1810 before the through-route
was finally completed.

Map continues on page 236.

The Kennet & Avon Canal was commercially successful for a while, but the building of the Great Western Railway in 1841 began to affect trade on the waterway. The railway company eventually bought the canal in 1851 and allowed it to decline through increased competition and poor maintenance. By 1910, commercial carrying had been reduced to local trading and by 1951 the waterway was officially closed. The Kennet & Avon Canal Trust formed in 1962 with the aim to return the canal to full navigation. This was finally achieved in 1990, with a re-opening ceremony by the Queen at Devizes Locks.

At first we will examine the eastern part from Reading to Devizes Wharf, which passes through some of the finest countryside in the counties of Berkshire and Wiltshire. Boaters should be aware that the Kennet Navigation, like the Thames, is a river navigation and may be susceptible to flooding after heavy rain.

Dunmill Lock near Hungerford.

Reading to Newbury

The junction between the River Kennet and the Thames is overshadowed by railway bridges, gasholders and a large supermarket. Terraced cottages and a waterside pub lead to Blake's Lock, which is controlled by the Environment Agency. The Riverside Museum is here, in a Victorian pumping station. It tells the story of Reading's two rivers and has a medieval mill wheel on display. Beyond the lock the next section was once dominated by Huntley & Palmers biscuit factory, which used the canal for bringing in raw materials, such as flour, and transportation of their finished products. A navigable backwater leads to Reading prison, made famous by former inmate Oscar Wilde who wrote *The Ballad of Reading Gaol* after being imprisoned there from 1896–1897.

As the navigation reaches High Bridge at Reading, the ownership of the waterway changes from being under the

Reading's High Bridge was built in 1787.

The Oracle shopping centre in Reading.

jurisdiction of the Environment Agency to that of the Canal & River Trust.

Boaters must observe a traffic light control at the bridge before entering the waterway through The Oracle shopping centre. This narrow 1,500-feet section has blind bends that could render it hazardous during flooding conditions, which is the reason for the traffic light control. Boaters are forbidden to moor up in The Oracle so potential shoppers need to find a mooring place above County Lock and walk back. The Centre has all the popular high street shops under cover, with cafes, bars and restaurants alongside the canal bank. It was formerly known as 'Brewery Gut' because it once passed though Simonds' Brewery, which closed down in the 1970s.

After County Lock, the navigation passes beneath a maze of ring roads and then through the residential outskirts of Reading to Fobney Lock. The navigation now edges into countryside, passing The Cunning Man pub, apparently named after a benevolent wizard. A number of flooded gravel pits can be seen alongside the waterway as it passes through Burghfield and Theale. Garston Lock, the last turf-sided lock on the Kennet Navigation, is followed by Sheffield Lock, which once had a turf-sided chamber but has been rebuilt with a scalloped brickwork edge. Then comes the first powered swing bridge on the navigation, which is operated by the boater.

The navigation continues alongside tree-lined water meadows, with the occasional lock and swing bridge to negotiate. Flooded gravel pits provide a refuge for wildlife or, in some cases, recreational areas for water sports. At Aldermaston Wharf in Padworth, a charming old cottage houses a Kennet & Avon Canal Visitor Centre as well as an excellent cafe. Aldermaston Station is close to the wharf, with trains to Reading and Newbury.

ABOVE **Operating instructions for the powered swing bridge at Theale.**

BELOW **Kennet & Avon Canal Visitor Centre at Padworth.**

ABOVE **Aldermaston Lift Bridge.**

BELOW **Widmead Lock being rebuilt in March 1990. The lock was the last to be restored before the navigation reopened in August that year.**

Padworth also has a large boatyard with a hire fleet. This is followed by an electrically operated lift bridge over a busy road, so boaters must ensure they know exactly what to do to work it, or risk being responsible for a long traffic hold-up. The bridge is followed by the scalloped-sided Aldermaston Lock.

After Aldermaston the navigation continues along the Kennet Valley, passing a large marina at Frouds Bridge to Woolhampton, where there is a waterside pub and restaurant. Locks appear about every half a mile and there are several swing bridges in the six-mile section between Woolhampton and Newbury. The navigation is mainly tree-lined and at times quite remote and peaceful, except when trains pass on the nearby railway. Monkey Marsh Lock at Thatcham is an example of a turf-sided lock, where the original chamber has been replaced by an ugly concrete and steel structure. Despite this, the lock has been listed as an ancient monument by English Heritage. Thatcham town centre with all its shops, pubs, banks and a railway station is close to the water.

A straight mile-long section leads to Widmead Lock, the last lock to be restored before the reopening of the waterway in 1990.

Near Widmead Lock, consider a visit to The Nature Discovery Centre, which is set around a lake just beyond the railway in Thatcham. There are waymarked paths, bird hides and a cafe.

The navigation now enters Newbury, where there are visitor moorings in the town centre at Victoria Park, opposite Newbury Wharf. Try to picture this scene 150 years ago, when Newbury Wharf was a complex of warehouses, workshops, stables and timber yards crammed with boats loading and unloading cargoes. Today's setting is so different, as most of the wharf has disappeared beneath car parks, leaving only The Stone Building as a memento of the wharf's

The Stone Building at Newbury Wharf.

John Gould

John Gould was a former working boatman and resident of Newbury who began a campaign to save the waterway when the local council threatened it with permanent closure. He took two narrowboats to Birmingham, returning to Newbury with loads of paving stone, proving the navigation could still be used. He began a petition to the Queen and collected 22,000 signatures opposing the proposed Act of Closure, which was withdrawn and never reached Parliament. His campaigning and organisation eventually led to the formation of the Kennet & Avon Canal Trust.

This plaque is erected as a "thank you" to
JOHN GOULD MBE
a resident of Newbury, founder member of
The Kennet & Avon Canal Trust,
and ex working boatman.
Without John Gould there would not be
a Kennet & Avon Canal today.
His efforts and energy are an example to everyone.
March 1997

The plaque in memory of John Gould, next to Newbury Lock.

commercial heyday. The old building has found new life as the Canal Information Centre and café, run by the Kennet & Avon Canal Trust. Inside, the main room has been renamed the John Gould Room in honour of the Newbury-based pioneer of the canal's restoration.

There is no towpath under the single-arched Newbury Town Bridge, so walkers must cross the busy main street to join the canal again. Boaters should be aware of strong cross currents between the bridge and Newbury Lock. This lock marks the end of the Kennet Navigation and the beginning of the Kennet & Avon Canal.

Newbury Town Bridge, built in 1770.

Newbury to Hungerford

The 57-mile-long Kennet & Avon Canal was built in 1810 by engineer John Rennie, who was also responsible for the Lancaster Canal, the Rochdale Canal and Waterloo Bridge in London.

Moorings above the lock at West Mills allow access to Newbury's main shopping streets and a large pub by the bridge. West Mills Wharf was once a hive of activity, with

A lovely section of canal near Kintbury.

coal being brought in for Newbury's textile industries (the main employers in the town for centuries). By contrast, today's biggest employer in Newbury is the mobile network operator, Vodafone. West Mills is an excellent place to linger awhile, with its row of old weavers' cottages, a converted mill and a swing bridge.

Continuing westwards, there are five miles of glorious remote countryside between Newbury and Kintbury. The only interruption is the noisy Newbury bypass, which was the centre of much controversy during its construction in the 1990s. Locks come at regular intervals, but all are set in the most beautiful locations surrounded by wooded hills.

Kintbury Lock has a station on one side, with The Dundas Arms pub and restaurant on the other. The pub is named after Charles Dundas, first chairman of the canal company in 1810, who also gave his name to the Dundas Aqueduct over the river Avon. Miss W Rennie, a descendant

Hungerford Wharf, with its trip boat and Town Bridge.

of John Rennie who built the canal, officially reopened the restored Kintbury Lock in 1972.

There then follows another lovely section where the railway is the only disturbance to the tranquillity of the canal, which now reaches Hungerford. Dun Mill, at the edge of Hungerford, is where the canal and the River Kennet finally part company. The town of Hungerford has a lot of charm with a number of antique shops and bookshops, along with plenty of pubs, cafes and restaurants. Be sure to try the Tutti Pole tea shop close to the Town Bridge. The waterfront is particularly attractive, with a line of old cottages facing the Kennet & Avon Canal Trust's trip boat mooring next to the Town Bridge.

Hungerford has two locks – the second of which is known as Hungerford Marsh Lock, and is unusual in having a swing bridge across the middle of the chamber that has to be moved before a boat can use the lock.

Competitors in the Devizes to Westminster canoe race, passing through Hungerford.

235

Hungerford to Devizes

At Froxfield the canal crosses the county border from Berkshire into Wiltshire. The countryside is open, with wide views of hills topped with woodland. Little Bedwyn is followed by Great Bedwyn, where the station is very close to the canal. Stop at Great Bedwyn Wharf to visit the village.

Nine locks at Crofton raise the canal to its short summit level. Here the focal point is Crofton Pumping Station, which houses two 19th-century beam engines whose job was to pump water from Wilton Water reservoir and feed it into the canal's summit level. One of the engines, built in 1812 by Boulton & Watt, is the oldest working steam engine in the world still in its original building and capable of doing its original job. The pumping station is open daily to the public from Easter to the end of September, and has a cafe and shop for visitors.

After the top lock at Crofton, the canal enters a wooded cutting before plunging into the 502-yard-long Bruce Tunnel. The tunnel has no towpath so walkers will need to cross over the hill. Burbage Wharf, at the western end of the tunnel, was once a busy place handling coal and agricultural produce. The wharf is located at the southern tip of Savernake Forest, once a royal hunting ground and now Britain's largest privately owned forest.

The short summit level ends with four locks at Wootton Rivers. The picturesque village is home to The Royal Oak pub and restaurant, and pretty thatched cottages. The church has a curious clock face made up of 12 letters instead of numbers, spelling out 'glory be to god'.

Now comes the Long Pound, which, for the boater,

ABOVE **A swan family on Wilton Water reservoir, at Crofton.**

BELOW **Crofton Pumping Station.**

The view from Honeystreet, with Woodborough Hill in the background.

provides 15 miles of lock-free cruising through the beautiful Vale of Pewsey. In practical terms the Long Pound is the sole provider of water for the 29 locks at Devizes as there are no reservoirs on this level.

There is The Waterfront Bar & Bistro on Pewsey Wharf, and The French Horn pub and restaurant is a short walk away from the bridge. Anyone needing shops will have to go to Pewsey village, half a mile away.

In the next 11 miles you pass through glorious countryside with no locks and just an occasional road bridge. Even the railway has disappeared to the south, having been a close companion since Reading. The canal gently winds around hills studded with sheep and wild flowers in summer, and the views are superlative on both sides of the waterway, with distant vistas of hillsides with ancient barrows and tumuli.

At first, after leaving Pewsey Wharf, a wooded section leads to an unusual cast iron suspension bridge at Stowell

Park. Then comes the elegant and ornamental Lady's Bridge at Wilcot, built in 1808 as an appeasement to Lady Wroughton, the local landowner, who objected to a commercial waterway passing through her land. She also insisted that the canal builders construct an artificial lake next to the bridge.

The delightfully named Honeystreet is overlooked by Woodborough Hill, with the Alton Barnes White Horse rearing up on the hillside behind the village. There has been a canalside sawmill at Honeystreet since 1811 and this is still in business, along with a country store. Honeystreet was once an important boatbuilding centre, making many of the boats and barges that operated on the canal. The Barge Inn, built at the same time as the sawmill, is one of the busiest waterside pubs on the whole canal. It will be another five miles before boaters and walkers find waterside refreshment at the next pub at Horton Bridge.

After Horton Bridge you gradually begin to leave the open farming countryside behind as housing and a large marina heralds the outskirts of Devizes. The canal enters a tree-lined cutting that eventually leads to Devizes Wharf.

practical information

Distance: Reading to Devizes Wharf is 53 miles with 55 locks and 1 tunnel.

Boaters: Boaters should be aware that the Kennet section between Reading and Newbury is a river navigation and could flood after prolonged rainfall.

Walkers: The railway closely follows the waterway as far as Pewsey. There are stations near and sometimes very near the canal at Theale, Aldermaston, Midgham, Thatcham, Newbury, Kintbury, Hungerford, Great Bedwyn and Pewsey. There is a continuous footpath throughout, except at Bruce Tunnel where walkers must go over the top.

Places of interest: Crofton Pumping Station, where there is the oldest working steam engine in the world, still in its original building and still capable of doing its original job.

Key pubs: The Bridge Inn at Horton Bridge; The Barge Inn at Honeystreet; The French Horn at Pewsey Wharf; The Dundas Arms at Kintbury; Lock, Stock & Barrel at Newbury; The Rowbarge at Woolhampton; and The Cunning Man at Burghfield.

The unusual clock face at Wootton Rivers Church.

Chapter 19

Passing through Sydney Gardens at Bath.

KENNET & AVON CANAL
WESTERN SECTION

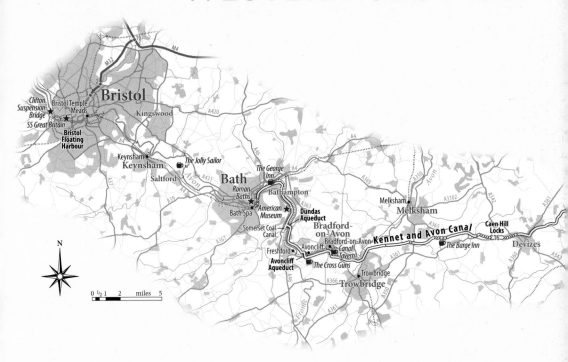

The final 40 miles between Devizes and Bristol contain most of the iconic landmarks of the Kennet & Avon Canal, beginning with the 29 locks at Devizes and two major aqueducts at Dundas and Avoncliff. The route also passes through Bradford-on-Avon and the city of Bath, before the navigation ends at Bristol's Floating Harbour. The journey begins in Wiltshire and then blends agreeably into the landscape of Somerset. After descending the Devizes locks the canal picks its way through gentle countryside before entering the Avon Valley. The scenery becomes progressively more dramatic as it approaches Bath where at first there are fine views over the city's rooftops before the Widcombe Locks drop the waterway into the Avon Navigation. The final section between Bath and Bristol is full of interest amid beautiful countryside.

Devizes to Bradford-on-Avon

The Kennet & Avon Canal Trust have their headquarters, information centre, museum, shop and cafe all together in a former bonded warehouse at Devizes Wharf. The Trust also operates a trip boat from a mooring place by the Wharf Theatre, which opened in 1979 within an old canalside warehouse. The annual Devizes to Westminster canoe race that takes place over the Easter weekend has its starting point opposite the theatre.

For boaters, liquid sustenance may be in order, for there is a lot of hard work to do with 29 wide-beam locks to negotiate in just over two miles. Luckily Wadworth Brewery and its visitor centre is also close to Devizes Wharf, and the brewery still uses Shire horses for short-distance deliveries.

The locks are split into three groups: 6 at the top, starting

Devizes Wharf with the Kennet & Avon Centre and a trip boat.

at Devizes Wharf, followed by 16 on the Caen Hill flight and another 7 at Foxhangers. The Caen Hill locks are close together on a steep hill, with very short pounds between each chamber. To store water each lock has a sideways extended side-pond. The Caen Hill Locks were the last to be completed in the original building of the canal by John Rennie and the last to be restored before the canal was reopened in 1990. Back-pumping was installed at Foxhangers in 1996, returning millions of gallons of water back to the top of the locks.

Completing the entire 29 locks without a break could take six hours and boaters are recommended to share the workload with another crew. A cafe strategically situated by the top lock of the Caen Hill flight offers a welcome rest for weary hands. Mooring is not allowed on the Caen Hill flight and operation of the locks works on a timetable that varies depending on the time of year. The locks are patrolled by a lock-keeper who may be persuaded to help inexperienced boaters.

ABOVE **Caen Hill Locks with prominent side pounds.**

BELOW **Boats leaving the bottom lock on Caen Hill flight.**

Foxhangers, at the bottom of the locks, has a boatyard and a marina, as well as moorings where boaters can recuperate after their exertions. The next place to stop is Seend Cleeve at the popular The Barge Inn, once the home of Fred Kempster, England's tallest man. At the time of his death in 1918 at the early age of 29, he was 8 feet 2 inches tall and weighed 27 stone. Today Seend Cleeve is an idyllic place to linger and ponder that it once was a centre for mining ironstone and had two blast furnaces with tramways leading to the canal near the lock.

The next section of canal features several swing bridges leading to Semington village and the junction with the now derelict Wilts & Berks Canal. This 51-mile-long canal opened in 1810 and connected to the River Thames at Abingdon via Swindon. The Wilts & Berks Canal was abandoned in 1914 and some of the line has been filled in. Nevertheless, the canal is slowly being restored by volunteers, aided by the Wilts & Berks Amenity Group.

Semington has two aqueducts: one built in 1807 over the Semington Brook, and a much grander version over a new road that was completed in 2004, and which required the canal to be diverted during its construction. Two locks at

The lock at Seend Cleeve, once the site of an ironworks.

Semington are the beginning of a pleasant lock-free five miles to Bradford-on-Avon.

About two miles from Semington is Hilperton, (a suburb of Trowbridge). Hilperton is a busy boating centre, with a large marina, two boatyards, shops and a pub near the road bridge.

As you leave Hilperton a high embankment with views of the River Avon is followed by a wooded cutting that takes the canal into Bradford-on-Avon. First there is a marina with a nearby pub before you reach Bradford Lock, where the Kennet & Avon Canal Trust have a shop and cafe. Just beyond the lock and bridge there is The Canal Tavern with a garden, followed by an ancient tithe barn. This is one of Britain's finest examples of a monastic barn, built in the 14th century, and it is open to visitors.

Take time to walk down the hill and visit the town, which is bisected by the River Avon. The river is crossed by a nine-arched stone bridge, originally built in Norman times but widened in 1769. It is one of only four examples of a chapel bridge left in Britain – the others are at Wakefield, Rotherham and St Ives in Cambridgeshire. The chapel, which was used by travellers in medieval times, later became a lock-up where drunks and troublemakers were left overnight to cool off.

Ancient tithe barn at Bradford-on-Avon.

Bradford~on~Avon to Bath

Now follows Avoncliff, the first of two superb aqueducts built in Bath stone over the River Avon. A thickly wooded section of canal arrives at a sharp bend leading to the three-arched aqueduct. The structure is overlooked by a pub, a cluster of old houses and a shop. During the 1980s, the aqueduct began to sag in the middle and needed restoration, which involved relining the canal bed with reinforced concrete.

The canal continues on a high wooded embankment overlooking the Avon Valley with the river and railway far below. This glorious stretch of waterway ends at Dundas Aqueduct, which is even more spectacular than its predecessor at Avoncliff.

Built in 1804, Dundas Aqueduct has classical columns, cornices and balustrades above three huge arches. This monumental structure spans the beautiful wooded Avon Valley, allowing boaters and walkers wide views in all directions. Named after Charles Dundas, the first chairman of the Kennet & Avon Canal Company, it remains as a magnificent tribute to engineer John Rennie.

The Avoncliff Aqueduct.

Brassknocker Wharf, at the end of the aqueduct, marks the junction with the former Somerset Coal Canal that once served collieries in the Radstock and Paulton areas south of Bath. The line, which has been closed for over 100 years, can be traced but only the first quarter of a mile is still in water and used for moorings. There is a boatyard and The Angelfish Restaurant at the end of the present line.

The next notable feature is Claverton Pumping Station, built to pump water into the canal from the River Avon. In its heyday it was powered by a huge water wheel pumping 77,000 gallons of water from the river every hour. Today, modern electric pumps do the work but the old pump is still operational and demonstrated to the public on special pumping days between Easter and September. Also worth a visit is the American Museum, which can be seen in Claverton village, a short walk from the canal.

The canal continues to follow the Avon Valley to Bathampton village, where by a waterside pub it takes a sharp turn to the west and begins the entry into the city of Bath. At first you see the city's rooftops above the Avon Valley and then you reach Sydney Gardens with its

Dundas Aqueduct.

RIGHT **Cleveland House Tunnel at Bath.**

ABOVE **Leaving Widcombe Bottom Lock to join the River Avon at Bath.**

RIGHT **Pulteney Bridge and weir at Bath.**

decorative footbridges. Next comes the short Cleveland House Tunnel, once the headquarters of the Kennet & Avon Canal Company. A trapdoor in the tunnel roof allowed clerks in the room above to exchange paperwork with the boatmen passing below.

Bath Top Lock marks the start of the descent to the River Avon by the seven Widcombe Locks. The superlative views surrounding the canal and across the city rooftops make this flight one of the finest in Britain. The final lock has a cavernous depth of nearly 20 feet as a result of two previous locks having been combined during restoration work in 1976. This bottom lock drops the canal into the River Avon and from now on you are on the Avon Navigation.

Boaters and walkers wishing to see more of the city should turn right at the bottom lock and follow the river to Pulteney Bridge. There are moorings on the approach to the bridge, and from here you can visit all the attractions the city has to offer, including Bath Abbey, the Roman Baths, the Thermae Bath Spa, the Jane Austen Centre, the Royal Crescent and Pulteney Bridge itself.

Pulteney Bridge was designed by Robert Adam and built in 1744. It is one of only four bridges in the world that is lined by shops on both sides. Trip boats operate above the weir on a section of the river that is out of bounds for visiting boats.

The River Avon and Pulteney Bridge at Bath.

Back at the bottom lock of the Widcombe Flight, boaters heading to Bristol will soon be aware that the canal has been replaced by a river navigation. The main features of this first section of waterway are a succession of bridges and a number of old warehouses, emphasising the amount of trading that once took place in this part of Bath. Moorings are available along this section and there are supermarkets, shops and pubs close to the navigation. After Weston Lock, the city's suburbs begin to recede and are replaced by wooded hills. At Newbridge there is a pub and a Park and Ride service into the city, and near it a marina with a shop as well as boating facilities.

Bath to Bristol

After Newbridge the city is left behind, and the navigation follows a series of bends into open countryside dotted with wooded hillsides. Kelston Lock, next to a marina and a pub, is a handy place to stop and visit Saltford village. A little further on, Saltford Lock has a beautiful setting with the remains of a brass mill and a popular pub called the Jolly Sailor overlooking the water. There is a sailing club here, so expect to see lots of yachting activity at weekends.

This beautiful section of river is known as the Avon Valley Country Park, and it follows a winding course to Swineford, where there is a lock, and then on to Keynsham. The waterside at Keynsham is dominated by the Somerdale

Sailing on the Avon Navigation at Saltford.

chocolate factory. Originally built by the Fry family to manufacture their chocolate, after Fry's merged with Cadburys and Cadburys was subsequently taken over by Kraft Foods, the factory was closed in 2011 and production moved to Poland. The future of the factory is likely to be demolition and the site being rebuilt with housing and a business park. That delicious smell of chocolate that once wafted across Keynsham Lock is, alas, no longer a feature of the region.

Next to Keynsham Lock the Lock Keeper pub has a petanque court in its garden. After Keynsham, the river takes a sharp bend to the north and arrives at Hanham Lock, in an attractive setting at the foot of a steep wooded hillside with a group of old cottages and two pubs. Here, the navigation becomes tidal and under the jurisdiction of Bristol City Council. Boaters can obtain a licence to cruise into Bristol from the waterway office at Hanham or from the lock-keeper at Netham Lock.

The tidal river passes along a steeply wooded valley to Netham Lock, which may be open or closed depending on the state of the tide. Here the navigation leaves the natural river and takes the artificial Feeder Canal into Bristol's Floating Harbour.

The Floating Harbour

The Floating Harbour was designed by William Jessop in 1809 to impound the tidal river, allowing ships to remain afloat while loading and unloading their cargoes. This was needed because the tidal rise and fall on the Avon can be as much as 40 feet, twice a day.

Bristol's prosperity was built on imports of such commodities as sugar, tobacco, timber and cotton. The ability of ships to work around the clock in the Floating Harbour gave rise to the phrase 'ship-shape and Bristol fashion'.

Canal boats and shipping co-exist in harmony at Bristol's Floating Harbour.

RIGHT **Bristol Cathedral.**

BELOW **SS Great Britain in Bristol Docks.**

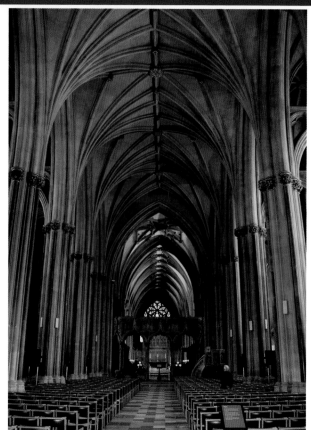

BRUNEL'S SS GREAT BRITAIN

The port closed in 1975 and the Floating Harbour has now been regenerated for leisure and residential use. Most inland waterway boaters find a mooring in the harbour and enjoy the many attractions of the city including the impressive cathedral. Visit Brunel's SS Great Britain, walk to the Clifton Suspension Bridge, visit Bristol Industrial Museum and the Arnolfini art gallery, then try some of the many pubs and restaurants that line the old docks.

One of the best mooring places is at Wapping Wharf by Bristol Industrial Museum, which was once an area of timber yards where the railway tracks have been preserved.

Bristol, with its many attractions, is an excellent place to end our great waterways journey and reflect on the wonderful, diverse scenery on this 780-mile-long loop around England's waterways. On this journey we saw the industry of the Black Country followed by remote wooded cuttings on the Shropshire Union Canal and high Pennine moorland leading into the city of Leeds. The narrow canals of the midlands contrasted with wide rivers such as the Thames and Trent and we visited ancient cities such as Oxford and Bath.

Clifton Suspension Bridge, Bristol.

practical information

Distance: Devizes Wharf to Bristol Floating Harbour is 40 miles with 50 locks, two aqueducts and two short tunnels in Bath.

Boaters: The 29 Devizes locks pose a real challenge. Boaters thinking about going beyond Cumberland Basin and the Entrance Lock at Hotwells into the tidal Avon must take advice and then think again as the journey towards the River Severn is potentially hazardous for small craft and a river pilot is essential.

Walkers: There is a continuous footpath throughout this part of the route until Netham Lock in Bristol, after which you have to complete the short journey into the Floating Harbour via the streets. The railway closely follows the navigation between Bath and Temple Meads in Bristol with a station at Keynsham. Between Bradford-on-Avon and Bath there is a station at Avoncliff. There are no stations between Bradford-on-Avon and Devizes.

Places of interest: There is lots to see and do in Bristol, including the Clifton Suspension Bridge Visitor Information Centre, and there are plenty of places worth visiting in Bath. The American Museum at Claverton and Bradford-on-Avon Great Tithe Barn are also worth a visit.

Key pubs: The Barge Inn at Seend Cleeve; The Cross Guns at Avoncliff Aqueduct; The Canal Tavern at Bradford-on-Avon; George Inn at Bathampton; the Jolly Sailor at Saltford.

Index